PENGUIN BOOKS
KASHMIR: THE UNTOLD STORY

Humra Quraishi is a freelance reporter and columnist based in Delhi. Her features and interviews appear in the *Times of India*, the *Hindustan Times*, the *Indian Express*, the *Statesman*, *Pioneer* and *Tribune*. Since 1990 she has been visiting Jammu and Kashmir regularly to report on the turmoil there and the effect it has had on the lives of the Kashmiri people.

'If you want to know how Kashmiris feel about India and the presence of the Indian Army in the Valley, you cannot do better than to read Humra Quraishi's [book]...Through her pen the Kashmiris talk to us. She has done as thorough a work of honest, unbiased reporting as I have ever read on the subject.'
—Khushwant Singh, *Free Press Journal*

'Humra Quraishi's book is driven by emotion, but is never over-emotional; it is honest, more than almost any other book on the movement; it is, indeed, one of the best books on Kashmir, ever.'
—*Hindustan Times*

'Quraishi's book is at its best when it details the many humiliations and privations Kashmiris have grown to accept as their lot...This is an affecting, informative book...a must read.'   — *Today*

'...a heartfelt narrative of the flip side of 13 years of turmoil in Kashmir...Too often the stories of everyday people get hijacked by jargon-driven analyses and political rhetoric. *Kashmir: The Untold Story* is a valuable contribution in dragging the focus back to them.'
—*The Indian Express*

'Quraishi has assembled a spectrum of interesting opinions from her extensive travels in the Valley...there are significant and sensitive insights into what has tragically befallen a peace-loving, tolerant, god-fearing society.'   —*Outlook*

Kashmir

The Untold Story

HUMRA QURAISHI

PENGUIN BOOKS

An imprint of Penguin Random House

PENGUIN BOOKS

USA | Canada | UK | Ireland | Australia
New Zealand | India | South Africa | China | Singapore

Penguin Books is part of the Penguin Random House group of companies
whose addresses can be found at global.penguinrandomhouse.com

Published by Penguin Random House India Pvt. Ltd
4th Floor, Capital Tower 1, MG Road,
Gurugram 122 002, Haryana, India

Penguin
Random House
India

First published by Penguin Books India 2004

12 11 10 9 8 7

ISBN 9780143030874

Typeset in Sabon by Mantra Virtual Services, New Delhi
Printed at Repro India Limited

www.penguin.co.in

Contents

Author's Note

Travelling through Kashmir during the assembly elections in late 2002, I met Father Jimborst, a Dutch missionary who has been working with the young people of the Valley for almost four decades, teaching at St Joseph's Higher Secondary School and Woodland School. We spoke outside the Holy Family Catholic Church on Srinagar's Maulana Azad Road on a September morning. Since he worked closely with young people, I asked him how the present generation differed from the younger Kashmiris of the past. After a long pause he replied, 'Once this was a beautiful, happy place. But now there is great sorrow. Look around and see for yourself, people are suffering so much that they've stopped expressing themselves ... [though] there's great tension and fear, no jobs ... It's like people suffering from cancer.'

This book is an attempt to document what the Kashmiri people have stopped talking about—the extent to which everyday life in their valley has become a struggle, at times an impossible one. These are stories we rarely hear because more dramatic, 'spectacular' tragedies like bomb blasts and shoot-outs get the headlines. There is little space available to highlight the daily humiliation Kashmiris suffer, the plight of families whose young men have disappeared, the effect of the long years of turmoil on the psyche of young and old alike, the changing nature of the family and faith and intercommunity relationships in the Valley, and the growing civic problems. This is the reason I have risked adding 'untold story' to the title of the book—so much is being written about Kashmir, but the deeper tragedy of a whole society being depleted in spirit is still little understood.

I cannot pinpoint the beginning of my special relationship with Kashmir. I remember the photographs of my parents 'honeymooning' in Srinagar in the autumn of 1953, which left a strong impression on me as a child. Perhaps the beauty and grace of the landscape communicated itself to a child even through the black-and-white pictures. In fact, for a long time I cherished the idea that I had been conceived on a walnut bed placed on the wooden floor and under the *khatamband* ceiling of a houseboat on the Dal Lake. My mother put an end to that fanciful thought—I was born some years after that, she said—but I never quite believed her at first. Years later, in the mid-1970s and 1980s, I went to the Valley as an adult and on each occasion it was like a homecoming. Then destiny brought me back again—this time not as a tourist. In May 1990, V.N. Narayanan, the editor of *Tribune*, asked me whether I would go to Srinagar and report on the situation there—after open rebellion against India erupted there in 1989, Kashmir was on everyone's radar. I agreed instantly.

That visit in 1990 was a turning point for me. Unthinkingly fashionable and flamboyant till then, I mellowed overnight as I saw scenes of disaster—at least impending disaster—all around. The army was everywhere; it was as if troops had been brought in to fight a war, except that they were ranged for the most part against unarmed civilians. Curfew had been imposed and life had come to a complete standstill; even those who had the means were unable to get essential commodities and few had access to health care and medicines in case there was an emergency. The people

I spoke to, even those I only saw from a distance in the streets, were all tense, angry and hurt. I heard a new horror story every morning when I ventured out of my hotel.

At the risk of sounding melodramatic, I have to say that nothing I had experienced before as an Indian had shocked, depressed and shamed me more. The faces and voices, both angry and anguished, of ordinary Kashmiris continued to haunt me long after I returned to Delhi. Thereafter, I visited the Valley regularly, reporting on the extreme hardship people faced, the changing socio-economic patterns, the human rights violations. It was a grim scenario, and things only got worse after 1990. Today, the turmoil and alienation may not be as immediately apparent as in the mid-1990s, but it is still there. The only difference is that people don't talk to you or demonstrate in the streets as readily as they used to. The anger, bottled up, is in fact more potent. It would be a folly to think that all that the Kashmiris have endured over the last decade and a half has not affected them. We can ignore the problem only at grave risk to our stability and reputation as a modern nation.

The first step towards any process of 'healing' is to accept the truth—that we have given the Kashmiri people much cause to feel alienated, and that some things have changed for the worse, and perhaps irrevocably so. The only sane and sensitive way to begin addressing the situation is by talking to the people of the Valley directly and with sincerity. You can tell them your side of the problem: over five decades have passed since the accession document, though with some loose ends, was signed; Kashmir breaking away from the Indian Union now would be fraught with danger and also unfair. What is feasible is greater autonomy, and talks to ensure concrete and planned development, more jobs, dignity for the Kashmiri people, and transparency, with a capital T. This last is perhaps most important because in the absence of transparency, all the money—and there has been a lot doled out by successive Central governments for Jammu and Kashmir—and laws are useless.

But I am no politician; I have no solutions to offer. The purpose of this book is to bring to as many people as possible all that I have witnessed during the last fourteen years in Kashmir. During these years things have changed radically for almost every person belonging to the Valley, whether a Pandit who had to flee his home, or was encouraged to do so by vested political interests, or a Muslim who has no choice but to stay in the Valley and suffer. As the Kashmiri artist Veer Munshi puts it, 'The horrendous events have reduced the status of the common Kashmiri to a label: secessionist, extremist, fundamentalist, militant, terrorist, migrant, refugee.'

Against this backdrop, there is talk again of talks between India and Pakistan and between India and a section of the Hurriyat that claims to represent the Kashmiri people (though as this book goes to press, in late February 2004, the talks with the Hurriyat are already in danger of being derailed after a few militant strikes—including an attempt on the chief minister's life—and excesses by the army). But the average Valley Muslim is cynical of such developments, caught as he is between the might of the state and the agendas of the militants. If only our politicians and planners cared to move beyond the helipads and heavily guarded hotels and interact with the men and women on the street, they might understand that no effort at a solution to the tragic situation in Kashmir can have any meaning unless the people of the Valley are directly involved in it.

I have seen and heard about too much pain in Kashmir. I have no illusions about the extent to which this one book can help lessen that pain. The book is as much for myself as for the Kashmiri people; it is one way of feeling a little less useless and helpless as a witness to great suffering. I remember the day at the Yateem Trust for orphans, run by doctors in Srinagar, when a young dentist, Rauf Mohi-u-deen, pushed the donation book in my direction. I had felt embarrassed and ashamed, for I had only a hundred-rupee note to offer. I had silently vowed that I would try and make up for it someday and I hope to do that through this book—all royalties will go towards relief for the women, children and men of Kashmir whose lives have been ruined by the turmoil.

In the writing of this book, I have been fortunate to have received invaluable guidance and support from Khushwant Singh, who encouraged me to tell the truth despite any possible unpleasant consequences; his own courage and forthrightness have inspired me tremendously. I was also informed and inspired by the uncompromising, well-researched and moving accounts of events in Kashmir by four remarkable journalists: Ajit Bhattacharjea, Muzamil Jaleel, Ayesha Kagal and Sukhmani Singh. I am also grateful to Ravi and Shantanu, my editors at Penguin India, for all their help, and to my several Kashmiri friends who shared their stories with me.

The Valley of Fear

It was a pleasant late September morning in Srinagar, in the year 2002. But the ease of the weather and the famed beauty of the landscape did not mean much any more; they hadn't for over a decade. I was returning to New Delhi with a sense of relief: the dreaded Special Task Force (STF) men had not barged into my hotel room at night, and no Kashmiri had accused me of being an agent of RAW or CIA or ISI—at least not to my face. I had been lucky.

In the coach taking us to the airport from the Tourist Reception Centre, my co-passengers were all grim-faced, a little nervous; before we could board the plane, we would be subjected to intense but often clumsy security checks at several points. Most of us knew the routine. We would be ordered to open every suitcase, and every piece of our clothing, including faded undergarments, would be patted and shoved around. As a general rule, all hand baggage is emptied out at three different places. And at each of these checkpoints there is a body search.

Till recently, it was routine in Kashmir for male cops and army men to frisk women. Mercifully that has changed, but only the previous evening the turf manager at the Royal Springs Golf Course, Nuzhat Gul Turay, was almost hysterical when she told me about the woman cop who frisked her at

Srinagar's Centaur Hotel: 'She touched and probed like a lesbian! It was so unnerving!' Didn't she think of complaining, I asked, given her important position—she was, after all, the turf manager of Farooq Abdullah's favourite golf course. Besides, her father was a prominent National Conference (NC) man from Shopian. 'I've complained so many times, about so many things! But nothing happens here ...The least that can be done is to install metal detectors and spare us this constant humiliation.'

So I didn't quite know what to expect at the first checkpoint to the airport. But the policewoman there went about her business in a brisk, businesslike, absolutely professional manner. And then just as I was about to walk on, she leaned towards me and said, 'What's this? This long thing here ... something's sticking out. In the last hijack ...'

'I'm having my menstrual period,' I whispered back.

'Madam, *chhotawala*—the smaller one ...'

'Terribly heavy flow ...' I began, but she pulled away, exclaiming, 'Ayyo!' and let me go through hastily, as though I was about to bloody her well-creased khakis.

The elderly Kashmiri woman behind me clearly posed no such threat. The second policewoman in the enclosure did a thorough check on her. She was made to take off her spectacles, chappals and socks. Her thin grey plait was untied (she might have been smuggling out saffron bulbs in her hair, perhaps?), she was asked to pull off her long dupatta, turn around, lift her kurta ... At the end of it all, she looked visibly shaken—obviously a first-time traveller.

The routine was repeated a short distance ahead. By the time we reached the third and final checkpoint, right at the terminal, the old lady was completely rattled. We both walked into the makeshift enclosure together, she looking bewildered, and before either of the two security women had said anything, she undid the drawstring of her shalwar and pushed it down, then stood still, her trembling arms held away from her body. There was pin-drop silence for a few seconds, before the security women recovered and nervously lifted the shalwar back to where it ought to be. 'This was the only place left to be searched ...' the old lady muttered absently in Kashmiri as she tied the string of her shalwar, 'so I thought ...'

Still muttering, looking lost and a little dishevelled, she boarded the plane ahead of me.

*

The city itself looks lost and dishevelled. Wherever you are in Srinagar, at whatever time, just stand awhile and look around to understand what the years of militancy and security operations have done to Kashmir. During one short walk down Maulana Azad Road in 2002, I saw a whole row of men standing hunched, waiting for their turn to be body-searched before they could proceed across the road; I noticed the unfinished building of the Human Rights Commission, under construction for four years, already looking like an abandoned shell; and at the decaying MLA Hostel building, I turned around.

To get a sense of how the atmosphere of suspicion, cynicism, fear and neglect affects the residents of the city, consider how it can affect even the visitor. The well-known television personality Karan Thapar wrote as recently as November 2003 about the shock of seeing Srinagar overrun by army tanks and the very special breed of commandos we have nurtured in India specifically to put the fear of God in ordinary citizens. 'As you step out of the airport,' Thapar wrote in his column in the *Hindustan Times*, 'you could be forgiven for thinking you've entered a city under occupation. Tanks and armoured cars surround the perimeter. Soldiers, with their guns held threateningly, stare at you. Wild-looking commandos ... drive menacingly past.' Ashok Upadhyay, Thapar's producer who hadn't been to Kashmir before, was stunned by the sight. '"The Kashmiri people must hate this," he said softly, staring all the while at the check posts with their evil-looking panels of metal spikes. "I can't believe there aren't better ways of doing this ..."'

The Indian Express of 16 March 2003 carried a report about a Japanese tourist, Koichiro Takata, who tried to kill himself shortly after he landed in Srinagar. He had arrived lured by the images of paradise sold in travelogues and tourist brochures about the Valley. 'What he saw instead was a bunkered city with helmeted and gun-toting security personnel far outnumbering the happy people he hoped to see ... depressed, the 22-year-old ophthalmology student tried to commit suicide yesterday .... Takata confessed that he went crazy and anxious thinking of the security surrounding him and stabbed himself several times with a pair of scissors.'

I have my own small story of coming undone. I was walking along the Bund, close to the Government Arts Emporium one afternoon when I heard sudden cries, followed by gunfire. Two boys had been shot dead the previous night by the BSF in the Maisuma locality (a JKLF stronghold) and I'd been told to be careful since there could be trouble during their funeral procession. I rushed into the gates leading to the emporium, along with several others. It was as if I'd entered a jail. The gates were shut, people were herded together like thieves, and a large, foul-mouthed security forces officer yelled repeatedly in a Bihari accent that nobody should move out without his permission and that there'd be hell to pay if any of us tried. Long after the cries outside had died down he refused to let anyone move. I tried talking to him and each time I was ordered back in the most obnoxious manner. By the third or fourth time this happened I'd had enough and screamed back that I had to be out, I was a reporter. The gates were finally thrown open by one of his men; someone grabbed me by the arm and pushed me out.

Even journalists, with their press cards and official permissions, have been through much worse in Kashmir, but that day it all seemed too much to handle and I sat down by the Bund and wept. I think I was there for close to half an hour. Passers-by glanced at me and walked on, no one stopped to ask what was wrong. In Kashmir today it is best to mind your own business.

*

Srinagar is a city under siege. It has been under siege, every single day, for nearly a decade and a half. People outside Kashmir read or hear reports of spectacular sorrows—half a village gunned down, bus passengers blown up, young men disappearing from home and often being found as disfigured corpses days or months later—and soon reach the inevitable stage where the news barely registers before they move on to the next page, a different channel. Horror fatigue has prevented any real understanding of what ordinary Kashmiris go through on a daily basis: fear, uncertainty, humiliation.

On the roads, scooters, cars, buses can be stopped just about anywhere and at any time. The vehicles will be searched, and the driver and passengers, too, and there will be no 'Please step aside' kind of civilized talk; there will be orders, some shoving around, some bullying, and sometimes a brutal thrashing. In July 2003, close to the time when noises about a new, enlightened approach to the Kashmir issue by the Government of India had begun, Tahmeena Yusuf, a teacher in a well-known college in Srinagar, was beaten up by BSF men because she did not allow their vehicle to overtake her car. By the time they were through with her, Tahmeena was barely able to stand. She was brought to the college in a semi-conscious state by her domestic help, and outraged students soon poured out onto the streets in protest.

On several occasions, travelling in the city by bus with a couple of male students, I watched helplessly as the bus was stopped at different checkpoints and the students ordered to stand in a huddle with the rest of the male passengers, while their luggage and bodies were searched. Mehbooba Mufti, vice-president of the People's Democratic Party (PDP) and daughter of the present chief minister, Mufti Mohammad Sayeed, told me, 'It is disgusting to watch grown men being made to do *uthak baithaks* [hold their ears and do squats as punishment] in full public view if they are found without their identity cards.' Little wonder that most Kashmiri men today walk about with a slight stoop. The insensitivity of those in charge of security can be stunning. Vijay Dhar, a prominent Kashmiri Pandit who chose to stay back in the Valley, told me that till 2001, at the Sonawar checkpoint (Sonawar, incidentally, is an upmarket area of the city) Kashmiri women were searched by security men. 'It was a shocking sight and I wrote very strongly about it,' he said. It was only after his intervention that female security staff were brought in. But status and position don't always count with the men in uniform. A senior bureaucrat told me of the time his car was stopped and his official driver, a young Kashmiri, pulled out and beaten up by the security men manning a check post as he watched helplessly. No explanations were given.

'This generation of Kashmiris has seen nothing but humiliation,' said Mehbooba Mufti. 'For the young, especially, New Delhi or GOI stands for crackdowns.' The well-known human rights activist Gautam Navlakha calls it 'dadagiri'. Going by the stories I heard from people whose homes had been searched by the army—on suspicion that terrorists were using them as hideouts—the dadagiri isn't restricted to the numerous checkpoints on the roads. When the army searches homes, often on flimsy evidence, entire neighbourhoods are ordered out into the open, where they must stay for hours. Recounting one such episode to me in the early 1990s, Mufti Bahauddin Faruqi, a former chief justice of Jammu and Kashmir, had fumed, 'The government is treating each person as a suspect. Even *India Today* says the total number of militants must be only about 600—though I say they are no more than 100—yet, to locate them a whole city's population is being hounded. The searches are done in the most brutal manner—even before dawn the whole area is cordoned off and loudspeakers keep blaring that everybody should come out of their homes. For the whole day after that the search goes on while entire families sit outside without food or water. Even women in labour are not allowed to move.' Things have only got worse over the last decade. Seventy-seven-year-old S.K. Dhar, a retired lieutenant colonel of the Indian army, was disgusted enough to lodge an official complaint in late 2001. 'I wrote to the corps commander about the attitude of the army ... I mean, it seems like an army of occupation. But I got no reply.'

If the policies of the Central government over the years have alienated Kashmiris, the security forces, it appears, have only made things worse. Thirty-eight-year-old Hameeda Bano, a senior faculty member of the English department of the

Kashmir University, is among the few non-political Kashmiris who are vocal about their anger against India. She comes across as a rebel at the very first meeting. 'It is a fact that India has colonized us,' she told me in late 2002. 'I feel passionately about this and I'm not afraid to say it. All the others feel the same but are cautious, otherwise they could be harassed ... We're a good example of what can happen—my house in the campus has been searched, my husband has had a FIR issued against him, even his mother, Munira Ahmad Khan, was arrested for twenty-eight days. But nothing will deter me from being outspoken. No Kashmiri today believes we were ever a part of India.'

Travelling in Srinagar and to the interiors of the Valley over the last thirteen years, I have heard stories of daily abasement over and over again. The demand for independence needs to be understood at this very basic level: in a land that has been their home for generations, people want the usual certainties of life that we take for granted, something as simple as crossing a street without being stopped and all but strip searched, or being brought down by an army jawan's or a militant's bullet. Caught between the Indian security forces and the terrorists trained and funded by Pakistan, a humiliated and terrorized people are in no mood to give in—not to India, not to Pakistan, not even to US mediation, of which they are deeply suspicious. A retired government official living in Shopian said to me, 'Kashmir is like a ping-pong game between India and Pakistan, with the US playing the referee.'

Different people express their bitterness in different ways. In the summer of 2001 one of the auto drivers who had taken me around the city told me that one should be wary of the Big Four—the American mind, Chinese arms, the Pakistani army and the Indian security forces. The following year it was another auto driver who told me pretty much the same thing, except that he also told me to beware of him. Amused by my reaction he laughed and explained, 'Because I'm going mad. I was settled in Nepal for years and then … I don't know what brought me back to this hell! Can't recognize a face. And all these army men—we can't understand what they want, they can't understand what we want!' Looking back at me, he almost shrieked, 'What we want is *peace*— just let us live in peace! Today our green Islam is becoming red!'

Startled, I asked if he was now hinting at some Chinese or other communist agency also working in the city, in addition to the Indian, Pakistani, American, and perhaps even the British, French and Russian.

He chuckled as though I had stretched my arm out and tickled the back of his neck. 'Communism *khallaas* … dead and gone. I've been to Nepal, I know everything about politics. No, red is blood. Today it is easy to kill here … thousands of unemployed boys sitting around with no jobs and no hope—they're ready to shoot and kill for just a few hundreds. Some of them will get caught, or the cops will arrest some passer-by. You see, here if A kills B, C is thrown behind bars for years to come. Sister, you kill me and—see that man there, that crippled beggar?—he will be arrested.' Almost immediately he shook his head, chuckled again and said, 'No, no, they won't arrest a crippled beggar, why would they arrest him, that's no use … they'll arrest some educated young man identified by the agencies as someone who might become prominent and raise his voice. Sister, visit the jails … just visit the detention centres and you will see I'm not talking rubbish …'

I wondered about this auto driver. He spoke well, but something about his voice, his chuckle, the manner in which he spoke and his eyes darted around suggested he was almost on edge. But this seems not so uncommon a condition in the city. Even when people do not speak about it you can sense in their posture and their eyes the strange mix of fear, uncertainty, panic, anger and sadness. I also found that older men had begun to leave home frequently for the psychiatrist's clinic, women spent much time on the prayer mat, and children had taken to playing war games fashioned around the violence in their society. I spotted several children playing hide-and-seek in graveyards—there were plenty of those around, practically one in every mohalla.

According to the psychiatrist Mushtaq Margoob, as many as ninety per cent of Srinagar's residents are emotionally affected by the long years of turmoil. But this internationally known psychiatrist has no plans to move out of Kashmir—'the valley of trauma', as many medical specialists have begun to call it. 'Why? Because I don't think I will be able to face Him if I go away now,' he said, pointing heavenwards. B.A. Dabla, a sociologist at Kashmir University, has no intention of fleeing either, and he minced no words when recounting instances of humiliation of even respected professionals and intellectuals by both the Indian security forces and the militants. The Greek political scientist Georgios Georgantas, who heads the International Committee of the Red Cross (ICRC) in Srinagar, was cautious, but confirmed what Dabla had said. Each time he visits jails and detention or interrogation centres, he told me, it 'affects' him. He chose his words carefully: 'The mental health of the detainees is a major concern. In fact, we have an Irish doctor on the staff here and he accompanies us whenever we visit jails and interrogation centres. Some detainees talk, some don't. Generally, it is the educated who find it very difficult to cope with the situation. They keep worrying about the amount of time they'll have to spend in these centres and how that might put them back in life.'

*

You can never be sure of anything in Kashmir, especially in Srinagar. What passes for information is propaganda unleashed by the Centre and the state government, and by Pakistan and the militant organizations. People are wary and suspicious of almost everyone—even, sometimes, people they are familiar with. There are constant rumours of several intelligence agencies operating in the Valley.

Most people open up only after checking on you. This was not always the case. In fact, in May 1990, when I had started reporting on the abnormal turn of events, people would bare their hearts and sometimes shout and scream, showing you where they had been hurt and how. I still recall the words of an angry young woman, Munira Khanum, whom I met in a shikara ferrying us across the Jhelum. 'What we've gone through is pure tyranny,' she had said. 'I've seen beards being pulled off, and fasting men being made to drink nullah water ...Yes, print all this with my name and photo!' (I quoted her in the report I did for the *Tribune* in the summer of 1990.) It was around the same time that Mufti Bahauddin Faruqi had said quite bluntly that he had no faith left in the system: 'Whom do we complain to? I don't expect any relief even from the President of India ... Can you imagine all Muslim judges being called subversives!'

Through the mid-1990s, however, I sensed things change. There was anger still, but it was a simmering rage not as readily expressed as before. Journalists were among the few unfamiliar people to whom residents would voice their opinions, but even this was rare. I can count on my fingertips the number of occasions when more than a handful spoke up about a public issue. One that I remember well might even seem anti-climactic: it was the time when a new concrete structure began coming up in place of the gutted wooden pagoda-style ziarat of the patron saint of the Valley, Nand Rishi Sheikh Nooruddin Wali, at Charar-i-sharief. In 1995, terrorists holed up in the shrine had set it on fire and retreated when the security forces surrounded it; and now the government was rebuilding it with no thought whatsoever to the history of the structure. Concrete was being used instead of the original wood, so that it couldn't be burnt down easily again! Explanations given by those in charge were hardly sensitive. The administrator of the construction, G. Moheiyuddin, told me, 'It will take another two years for the structure to be complete. The concrete building will have a covering of wooden panels to give the original effect ...' This was hardly reassuring for the Kashmiris, to whom the shrine is an integral part of their culture and religious beliefs. A Srinagar-based medical student, Basharat Ahmad, who was visiting the shrine after a gap of ten years, kept exclaiming that he could not relate to the new structure: 'This building is so different in style and design ... And concrete! How can they do this? How will I come here now? It isn't the same place any more. Everything has changed!'

Many other changes were becoming visible through the late 1990s. There was a sense of despair, and people were beginning to accept harsh realities and make compromises. Travelling around in the Valley during that period, interacting with families, I discovered that young boys were being sent to Delhi or Bangalore or even the US for studies. And subtle inquiries were being made by many families for matrimonial alliances outside the state for their daughters, which was unheard of till then since the average Kashmiri always believed that he came from a better stock than the Muslims of Uttar Pradesh, Madhya Pradesh or Bihar. The results weren't always happy. 'After they are through with class ten we have to send them [the boys] out of this place if we want them safe and to have any kind of future,' a father told me. 'Not that all goes well for them there—they have problems adjusting, and people in those cities don't always welcome them. They are treated with suspicion and distrust.' The girls who married outside the state also found it difficult to adjust and quite a few suffered unhappy marriages. Yet, people felt that was the price they would have to pay, for they saw no hope of a decent life in the Valley.

That fear of sons being picked up continues to grip most families even today. Whenever young students accompanied me on my travels through the city and to the outskirts, the boys would make it a point to call home—particularly their mothers—if it seemed that we wouldn't return before sunset. The fear is not without a reason. There are more than 6000 young men missing in the Valley, all of whom, according to the lawyer-activist Parvez Imroz who heads the Association of Parents of Disappeared Persons (APDP), were picked up for interrogation and never came back. No one knows which jail they are languishing in, or if they are even alive. The co-founder of the association is a middle-aged mother, Parveena Ahangar, whose teenaged son Javed was picked up by the National Security Guards from his Batamaloo home on 18 August 1990 and remains untraced. I met Parveena briefly and for days her face haunted me: almost passive, tears welling in her eyes, as she recounted precise details of what had happened that day and all the days and evenings she had spent visiting jails to locate her son. Almost twelve years later she still did not have the courage to give up hope and confront the terrible possibility that Javed might never return. 'Sabr,' she kept saying softly every now and then through the time we spoke. *Sabr*. Patience.

Zahir-ud-din, associate editor of the Valley's leading English daily, *Greater Kashmir*, has written a book on these missing young men—*Did They Vanish In Thin Air?*. For a while he also wrote a fortnightly column in his newspaper on human rights violations in Kashmir. Till Farooq Abdullah's National Conference government presented him with a choice: either he discontinued the column, or the state government withdrew all its advertisements. The newspaper had to survive, so the column did not.

*

In 2002, I saw the most visible change of all in everyday family life. There were actually fewer homes than before. House after house, of ordinary civilians, was a mere burnt-out shell, and yet there was nothing beyond a pathetic compensation by the government and no public outburst. Over dinner at a senior bureaucrat's home—whom many in the media refer to as the self-proclaimed viceroy—I was appalled to hear the man explain calmly that they (the establishment) had no choice but to burn down structures, either on grounds of suspicion that terrorists were holed up in them, or in sheer retaliation. This was unavoidable, it wasn't their fault. I remember wondering if he truly had no idea what these acts—and the grudging compensation that never went over a few thousands—were doing to society. All seemed quiet on the surface, but the rage was there, barely contained in so many minds, and building up. Didn't that frighten him?

The hatred among ordinary Kashmiris for the sarkari folk can be judged from this small, seemingly insignificant incident. While in Srinagar I would often stop at a particular handicrafts outlet and chat with the salesmen. Talk would invariably centre on my impressions as a journalist, the places I had been visiting, the people I had been meeting. They would also tell me about their day-to-day, even personal problems. Till the day they saw me talking to a well-known government official with whom I had some friends in common. I hadn't sought him out; he had just happened to pass by that shop while I was there. The next day the salesmen didn't hurl abuses at me, but they asked me no questions either. They stuck to the usual formalities and said nothing more than was absolutely necessary. They were still civil but it was clear they had shut me out. That was the end of our chats.

Everyone I met that autumn in 2002 was guarded. Only when they were absolutely certain that I represented no intelligence agency would they talk. 'The Indian government has unleashed many people here in different guises,' one man told me, 'how do we know you aren't one of them?' Unlike in previous years, you couldn't really move around alone and go into lanes and by-lanes asking people how they were faring or about the violations they had been subjected to. I have a long list of people who agreed to meet me and at the last minute declined to give an interview.

Most days the cops were everywhere, keeping a watchful eye on you, even while you sat reading a book or sipping tea in one of the few operational restaurants. This was especially true of the Broadway's coffee shop, Coffea Arabica, which opens onto Maulana Azad Road. The road has quite a number of important establishments, like the MLA Hostel, on it— and therefore a good number of Maruti Gypsies and other police vehicles too (many of these without number plates). Given their presence, it did not surprise me that people I met at Coffea Arabica were reticent to the point of seeming rude, even hostile. At the garden restaurant by the Bund—Tao's

Café—I was told by the proprietor, Hussain sahib, that a group of doctors and engineers met every Friday afternoon after juma namaaz and that I should come over and interview them. The next Friday afternoon when I landed there, this group of seven to eight men all looked taken aback and initially refused to talk. Eventually, one of the leading paediatricians of the city, Dr Altaf Hussain, who was part of the group, agreed to speak to me, his answers interspersed with the refrain 'These days one doesn't know who's who'. The others, too, asked me several times to repeat details about myself and my work before they actually spoke, but even then they were very cautious and didn't bother to disguise the look in their eyes that made me feel unwelcome.

But this book wouldn't have been written if I had been sensitive enough to be hurt by such looks. Or by brusque orders or the constant rumours. Or by the fact that I had to survive on a tight budget while travelling with other journalists in rural Kashmir during the days leading up to the now famous 2002 elections that brought Mufti Mohammad Sayeed to power. It wasn't the most comfortable of times, moving about in erratic buses, in rickety auto-rickshaws or simply walking, sometimes for over an hour. And then, of course, wherever I went, there was the wall of distrust and wariness that couldn't always be breached. That, more than anything else, depressed me deeply and it took some effort to get on with the job.

The army and police personnel, I discovered, were suspicious too. Of everybody. I visited the Government Hospital for Psychiatric Diseases five times over two days to try and meet Dr Mushtaq Margoob for an interview, and each time the BSF jawan there stopped the young man accompanying me to ask the same questions. The young man was equipped with his 'life saviour'—the identity card that every Kashmiri is required to carry—otherwise he could easily have found himself in the Central Jail, which is in any case an extension of the lone hospital for psychiatric diseases in the Valley. I was questioned too, the first time, while the jawan rolled himself a beedi, looking at me closely to figure out my status. Journalists seemed fine by him, but it was the phrase 'from New Delhi' that finally reassured him. He lit his beedi as I moved on through the 'Kaathi darwaza', and I could sense him following me with his eyes till I turned the corner towards the gurdwara located not too far from the gate.

The army men, perennially on guard, short of sleep, on duty in a place where few want them and where their own lives are in danger every hour of the day, are not in the best of mental health. A casual conversation with Father Johnson Thomas, the vice principal of the prestigious Burn Hall School in Srinagar City, resulted in an unexpected and unsettling discovery. Father Johnson told me of a Christian jawan—about whom he would give me no details, of course—coming to him for confession. The Father expected the usual—the all too common surrender to the needs of the body during a long posting away from the family. But the guilt-ridden jawan sounded too disturbed for someone who had only had a one-night stand. The Father coaxed him to unburden himself. And the jawan told him about being ordered by his commanding officer to kill a man they had captured, a suspected militant. He kept asking Father Johnson what he should have done—should he have listened to his boss, or to the voice of God? Where did his duty lie? He had no choice, he said, he was only following orders. In Father Johnson's opinion the man was seriously disturbed. He doubted if the army recognized that he needed counselling. It frightened me to think of emotionally disturbed, psychologically damaged men like him being charged with guarding millions, a majority of whom had no love to offer him.

During the elections in late 2002, the group of journalists I was with stopped at a polling booth in Kakapora in the Pulwama district one afternoon. In the tent adjoining the polling booth, I saw a thirty-something CRPF jawan praying before a makeshift mandir. It was a touching, heart-warmingly normal sight that I hadn't seen in all my recent travels through the Valley: he had forgotten the fear of terrorist strikes, he had forgotten the need to intimidate or warn. He had put away his gun and sat cross-legged, his back to anyone who might want to attack him, in a posture of complete surrender to his God. Suddenly it seemed as if all was not lost in the valley of fear. I walked to his tent. When he finally noticed me, he turned around, got up when I nodded and moved away, thinking that perhaps I wanted to offer my prayers to the deity as well.

It had been a long time since I'd had any army or police person in Kashmir looking at me with anything other than barely suppressed suspicion or the cold indifference of a professional with a job to do. We began talking, and I was surprised by how easily he talked to me and how much. He told me that he missed his wife and daughter whom he had left behind in Karnataka, he told me of his village and how he longed to go back. He loved children, he said, and wanted to befriend the children in this village, but he had to be cautious and keep his distance—what if the children themselves or their families heaped terrible allegations on him? He knew people here did not trust him because of his uniform.

Had he tried, I asked. 'No, madam, there is no one we can talk to here.' Was it because he beat up the villagers? Army men were known to do that. He looked baffled. But why would he do that, he asked. 'I never touch their hens and cocks! Pure vegetarian ... I don't need those things. It's the RR men who do the beatings.'

Did he feel lonely, I asked, and he was silent. What about his biological needs, as a man? This time he looked shocked and shook his head vigorously. 'Tell me, madam,' he said, not looking at me, 'you are a reporter, you are on duty here ... so you can't think of all this. We are also on duty here ... everything is under control.'

I thought of embarrassing him a bit, asking exactly what was under control—the situation in the Valley or his needs— but I had derived much comfort from the exchange and didn't want to ruin it. For one afternoon the jawan from Karnataka had restored some of my lost faith in governments, security forces, in ordinary men. Our little conversation had been all the more remarkable because army personnel rarely talk to strangers, especially to journalists. It is a hard life for them too: nothing in their training equips them for fighting wars within the borders of their own country, often against people who they have been told are fellow Indians; it does not equip them to fight terrorists who operate from among innocent civilians; and it certainly does not equip them to meet the hostility of a disaffected population with understanding and maturity. Most of the jawans and officers, for instance, know next to nothing about the Kashmir problem and the genuine grievances of the Kashmiris.

*

The affluent are rarely affected drastically by turmoil and hardship, and from visible evidence, at least, that appears to be the case in Kashmir as well. I was told otherwise by two of the Valley's richest men one morning. I met them at the Royal Springs Golf Course. Gulzar Hussain (of Shaw Brothers) and Moheiyuddin Khanday came for the interview straight from a game of golf, and I couldn't help asking whether they played golf there only to get closer to the political elite (the chief patron of this course was the then chief minister Farooq Abdullah). Khanday made a long face at this, and Hussain retorted, 'It is easy for you to say these things. Do you realize how hard things are for us? While you would eat eggs and toast for breakfast, I have to pop all types of medicines first thing in the morning to survive in these tense times. I'm only in my mid-forties but I have seriously high BP and what not ...we play golf to release tension!' Neither wished to go into details about the 'tense times' nor confirm or deny stories about militant groups harassing the rich. A leading businessman had said to me, '*Hum logon ko bhi Pandits jaise yahaan se bhagna tha*! [We should have fled too, like the Pandits.]' Some have indeed shifted base to New Delhi, unable to satisfy the demands made by several militant outfits.

Flight is an option for anyone who can afford it. Life outside the Valley can only be better, after all. People from every section of Kashmiri society, irrespective of class and religious status, often toy with the idea of moving out. Many Kashmiri Pandits are already refugees in Jammu, Delhi and other cities of north India. But for Kashmiri Muslims, especially, life outside is not easy; and many are unable to cope. Rauf Rasool, an extremely tense-looking teenager summed it up for me: 'When my mother shifted me from here to Pune, so that I could study in a supposedly safer environment, I was teased and called "kharku" [militant]. And now I am back, being called a dog by the security forces.' In Delhi, all Kashmiris who visit are required to report at the nearest police station before checking into a lodge or guest house. Little wonder then that most guest houses do not want them—their Muslim name, Kashmiri features and a Valley address could land the proprietor in trouble with the local police. A slim booklet brought out by a PUDR (the People's Union for Democratic Rights) team in early 2002, after receiving reports of harassment of Kashmiri Muslims in Delhi, says:

There are no official records available of the number of Kashmiris who visit Delhi, but it is estimated that nearly two lakh Kashmiris reside in Delhi. Of these, more than half are here between September and March. Many of them live in one- or two-room tenements, paying a higher rent than what others would have to pay for the same accommodation .... Rather than provide specific individual cases of harassment this report merely seeks to highlight the nature of the problems encountered by them in the course of their search for livelihood .... Even before they leave J&K they are aware that they will be met with hostility and suspicion. But nothing they have heard before or stories that have been told to them prepare them for the actual encounter with India ...

We met scores of families in the localities of Lajpat Nagar, Bhogal, Pant Nagar, Batla House and Old Delhi over three weeks of January. It emerged that the main problem encountered by Kashmiri shawl and carpet sellers in particular is one of police harassment which has become worse since September 11 and peaked after December 13. The police now feel more emboldened to stop Kashmiris whenever they are out on their rounds. Most Kashmiris ply on bicycles and two wheelers, a few in cars. They are asked to produce their identity papers etc 'to the satisfaction of the police', failing which they are taken to the local police *thana* for questioning ... Children are discouraged from playing in the neighbourhood parks. Two young boys who ventured out one evening were accosted by a group of boys who began to abuse them and accuse them of being 'enemy agents'. When they replied they were 'Kashmiris and not terrorists', they were beaten up ...

The fear and uncertainty of Kashmir follows them no matter how far away they go from Kashmir in India. Recently, strolling along Kovalam beach in Kerala, H.K. Kaul, chief librarian at Delhi's India International Centre, spotted a shop selling Kashmiri carpets and artefacts and walked in. A Kashmiri Pandit who moved out of the Valley way back in 1965, Kaul has always been nostalgic about his home. 'I saw a very young Kashmiri Muslim boy working there and began talking to him in Kashmiri. The boy's face turned pale and he stared at me, speechless. I was taken aback by his reaction. Perhaps he thought I was an intelligence man come to arrest or hound him all the way from Srinagar ... This degree of fear in the young generation saddens me.'

*

After I returned from the Valley in late 2002, it took me a while to start writing this book. The terrorist strikes, the extreme human rights violations by the security forces—it is simpler to write about these things; but how do you convey the less visible, less spectacular tragedy of the wasting away of a society? It is like a slow, stubborn poison in the bones. What I had seen and sensed was too depressing. Kashmiri society might recover, but I felt then and still do that something vital will have been lost forever.

Also, close friends, well wishers and Kashmir watchers asked me to think twice before I proceeded. They told me not to dismiss lightly the implications of criticizing the Central government, especially the present government with its strong right-wing agenda. The official propaganda about Kashmir and Kashmiris—which most Indians outside the Valley, enraged and terrified by news of terrorist strikes, readily believe—is indeed strong. I realized how much damage it can do when some Kashmiri Muslim friends asked if they could stay with me in Delhi and I hesitated. Would it land me in some problem with the police? This apprehension wasn't at all far-fetched. Earlier that year, a serving police officer from Jammu and Kashmir had been picked up by the Delhi police from the upper-middle-class area of Vasant Kunj, only because he looked like a Kashmiri, had a Muslim name and a Valley address. It was later discovered that he was in the capital on an official visit, and was let off; but what would have happened had he been a student or a lecturer or a shawl seller? Or even a journalist? A non-controversial journalist like Iftikhar Gilani of *Kashmir Times* had been detained for seven long months in New Delhi's Tihar Jail on bogus charges, then released without any apologies offered or even an acknowledgement of the serious nature of the blunder.

Given these examples, my hesitation over hosting my Kashmiri Muslim friends was only natural, if more than a little shameful. Of course, no such thought crossed my mind when, shortly afterwards, a Tamil Hindu friend from Bangalore stayed in my apartment. This kind of attitude is more than half the problem when it comes to Kashmir. This divide, the distrust and callousness, will ensure that the army remains in Kashmir, doing badly what it was never trained to do in the first place. It might even ensure that we finally lose Kashmir.

By the end of April 2003, when I was working on the final draft of the manuscript for this book, the new PDP government, supported by the Congress, was beginning to take some positive steps to address the mess in Kashmir. Mehbooba Mufti had formally asked the home ministry to probe cases of the missing young men in the Valley, and to check the witch-hunt directed against Kashmiri students studying outside the state, in Uttar Pradesh, Uttaranchal, Maharashtra and Punjab. She had also filed cases against some security officers accused of abuse of power. But most people in the Valley feel that the damage done over thirteen years has been too serious and widespread; it would require a full-fledged, almost superhuman effort to undo its effects.

I think this may be beyond the ability of the present crop of leaders. For all those who think things can be changed in a hurry, here are a few facts:

• Over 70,000 Kashmiris have lost their lives due to the turmoil in the Valley in the last fourteen years. Government estimates don't go beyond 25,000. The veteran journalist Prem Shankar Jha, writing in the *Hindustan Times* of 11 October 2002, gives a break up—even going by the government estimate of 25,000 Kashmiris who have been killed since 1990, he points out that 'three-fifths of them were either militants or supposed militants, killed by the security forces, or innocents killed in "crossfire". Kashmiri estimates run far higher. Nearly all of them were young ... There is a martyr's graveyard in every mohalla of a town and in every village, and an entire generation of young men and adolescents has grown up on the stories of their heroism and sacrifice'. This is something we tend to forget in the hype and knee-jerk optimism that follows any 'Kashmir package' that the government announces. Almost every Kashmiri I have spoken to in the Valley—from separatists like Shabir Shah and Yasin Malik to students and housewives—has said to me, 'We've had 70,000 to 80,000 martyrs to the cause ... there can be no going back now.' And there are far too many who would agree with what M.A. Untoo, a separatist leader, said in response to my query about why their struggle couldn't have been a non-violent, Gandhian struggle. 'Not in these circumstances,' he had said. 'We don't have a leader [like Gandhi], and then each one of us has witnessed killings—members of my own family have been killed. I have filed 604 complaints with the Human Rights Commission but no action has been taken. So tell me, what do we do?'

• More than 6000 young men remain untraceable in the Valley after they were picked up for interrogation by the security agencies. The leading human rights activist Balraj Puri wrote in the *Indian Express* on 27 October 2003: 'The state government has conceded in the state assembly that the number of missing persons from 1990 to December 2002 stands at 3744. The Association of Parents of Disappeared Persons [APDP] claims that it has registered over 7000 cases. It has further alleged that 84 persons have disappeared since the present government [the PDP government of Mufti Mohammad Sayeed] came to power.' Custodial deaths haven't stopped either. This new government has ordered magisterial inquiries, but none of the cases has been reported to the National Human Rights Commission (NHRC). It is shocking that while it is mandatory for the superintendents of police and deputy commissioners in all other states of the country to report incidents of custodial death to the NHRC, this is not required in J&K. But as Balraj Puri asks, pertinently, why should this prevent the Mufti's government, so committed to the 'healing touch' policy, from reporting the cases to the NHRC anyway?

• Three lakh educated people are currently unemployed in Kashmir. According to an August 2002 report, there were only 11,200 business establishments in Kashmir—a 32 per cent drop from 1989.

• The agriculture sector was once the mainstay of Jammu and Kashmir's economy. Today, the state's annual food grain production is estimated at just over 13.5 lakh tonnes. This is well below its actual requirement, and approximately Rs 400 crore is spent annually on importing food grains. The consumer goods industry in the state is virtually non-existent. The state's traditional industries—the silk and shawl industry, carpet weaving, wood carving—have taken a beating over the last thirteen years of violence. Despite what the official media and even, surprisingly, the independent print and electronic media tells us, tourism is still down. And while experts believe that the state has the potential to generate around 16,000 MW of hydroelectricity, it only generates 800 MW. Add to all this the massive corruption that continues to plague the administration, and it is clear that no one has been thinking seriously about development in J&K.

• A Médecins Sans Frontières report states clearly that 'the violence in one way or another has touched each family living in Kashmir and this is having a profound effect on the overall well-being of the people here … in Kashmir most people have … psychological problems'. As a bewildered relief worker had put it movingly: 'It is as if a whole population is suffering from cancer … a cancer of the mind.'

A bold, honest vision is required to pull Kashmir out of chaos, and people need to work together to do this. How can any of this happen in a society that continues to be humiliated and terrorized every single day, and where fear and insecurity have made every man and woman suspicious not just of the establishment but also of each other?

A Troubled History

Towards the end of 2002, about a month after I returned to New Delhi from Srinagar, I ran into JKLF's Yasin Malik and his aide Masoodi at a party in south Delhi. What began as the usual pleasantries soon turned into a heated discussion when Yasin brought up the subject of Kashmiri independence. I asked him if he had ever considered how this independence, even if it were possible, would affect the Indian Muslims; one Muslim nation carved out of the country in 1947 had played enough havoc with the community's sense of security and had given the Sangh Parivar ample ammunition with which to target Muslims. Yasin retorted that I was mixing up issues, that independence for Kashmir and the status of Indian Muslims could not and should not be connected.

The artist Satish Gujral, brother of the former prime minister I.K. Gujral, joined us, and our exchange prompted him to recount what Jawaharlal Nehru had told him almost five decades ago. 'The year was 1956,' he said, 'and I was painting Panditji's portrait. The sittings were spread over a month, and Inder often accompanied me. I'd recently returned from Mexico and New York where I'd heard a lot of talk about the Kashmir dispute, and I remember asking Panditji why we were spending so much money and time trying to retain Kashmir even in the face of international criticism. He told us that shortly before both the Congress and the Muslim League agreed to the Partition, Jinnah had suggested a federation of Muslim-majority states which should be given autonomy. This was rejected. Later, when they agreed on the Partition, Jinnah said that these states should accede to Pakistan, implying that only non-Muslim-majority states could be part of India. Panditji said that he refused to agree to this, for the simple reason that Muslim-majority states in India would automatically guarantee safety for Muslims in other parts of the country where they were in a minority. So you see that was the rationale in keeping Kashmir. Panditji told us that though Patel wanted Kashmir to go, he saw to it that we retained it.'

And Nehru's position must have been strengthened, I said to Gujral, by the fact that the threat to Muslim-majority Kashmir around this time came from a group of Muslims. I was referring to the state's invasion, soon after the Partition, by Afghan raiders widely believed to have been sent by Pakistan. Gujral shook his head and said emphatically, 'It is absolutely wrong to even suggest that Jinnah sent those invaders. I know for a fact that the English Governor General of the North West Frontier Provinces who was extremely anti-Congress was behind the entire move.' How could he be so sure of this, I asked. 'Don't forget that we hail from Jhelum. My father, Avatar Narain Gujral, was a member of the Constituent Assembly. We had converted our home into a refugee camp during Partition and those invaders made it their first target. I must have been around twenty years old and remember each detail, it's a nightmare that haunts me even after all these years. It was definitely the British who sent those Afghans in, not Pakistan.'

I found this interesting: what he was saying could give

the subcontinent's recent history a new twist and perhaps help towards saner negotiations over Kashmir. It could, but of course it wouldn't. It is unlikely too many Indians today will believe Gujral's version—no politician or bureaucrat will—and the point is not whether it is factually correct or incorrect. There is a long history to the Kashmir issue that needs to be understood, but history has always been hostage to prejudice and ideology, and of late religion has begun to colour everything, further complicating an already complex issue. As the octogenarian Kashmiri scholar Agha Ashraf Ali, poet Agha Shahid's father, said to me, 'Indian history can never be written impartially and truthfully unless, when we begin to write it, we forget that Aurangzeb was a Muslim and Shivaji a Hindu.'

Whatever the intention of whoever it was that sent the Afghan raiders, the invasion finally pushed Maharaja Hari Singh to sign the instrument of accession to India in a hurry and Indian troops went in to drive the invaders out of Kashmir in October 1947. Most Kashmiris today will tell you that accession to India was a decision that an unpopular ruler took; the people of Kashmir never accepted it. Whether this was always the case or something that disaffected Kashmiris have now convinced themselves about is immaterial. The situation in the Valley, at least on the surface, may seem better now than it was in the early 1990s, when there was open revolt, but it would be a grave mistake to ignore the simmering resentment and disgust. If you are observant enough, you will see it in the eyes of the average Kashmiri. Agha Ashraf Ali traces the seeds of this great discontent to Partition. 'The main culprit is Partition, which was a political and economic absurdity,' he said categorically. 'And yes, there's no doubt that Kashmir is the unresolved issue.' Had Sheikh Abdullah been allowed to do things his way, he believes, the situation might have been different. 'Sheikh Abdullah couldn't succeed because the home ministry couldn't stomach his popularity—and let me say that in this the five per cent Kashmiri Pandits who were the educated lot acted as conspirators and were responsible for causing a rift between Nehru and Abdullah. Nehru's private secretary Dwarka Nath Kachru played a dubious role.'

Journalist turned diplomat and member of the Rajya Sabha, Kuldip Nayar is also of the opinion that Nehru may have won Kashmir for India in 1947–48, but 'messed' up the situation in the Valley in 1953 when he decided to dismiss and arrest Sheikh Abdullah and replace him with Bakshi Ghulam Mohammad as Kashmir's prime minister. 'I'd met and known Sheikh Abdullah and till that time he had no problems with New Delhi. In fact, he used to always stress on building a secular state. He was never in favour of an Islamic set-up. The problem started in 1953 with the Sheikh's exit, though it actually erupted only after the elections of 1987 which were blatantly rigged. Yasin Malik told me that after he witnessed the rigging he decided to replace the ballot by the bullet.'

Yasin Malik himself, and politicians like Muzaffar Baigh and even the present chief minister, Mufti Mohammad Sayeed, had in earlier interviews told me exactly the same thing. As had Mir Qasim, the controversial former chief minister who assumed office in the early 1970s. For some years now Qasim has made New Delhi his base. When I met him for the first time in 1990, he was staying in a cramped government quarter just off the Jor Bagh market in south-central Delhi. He now lives in a bungalow in Lodi Estate allotted on the freedom fighters' quota (though he makes it a point to stress that he has another house in Srinagar where he spends the long summer months).

Armed J&K police personnel guard the gates, protecting the elderly Mir Qasim and his wife, and, when I met him in January 2003, also their young grandson who was visiting from the US. Mir Qasim looked sad and depressed and was not in a mood to dwell much on today's politics.

When I asked him to pinpoint the causes that have led to the present level of turbulence in his home state, he mentioned 'the 1953 incident of Sheikh Abdullah being humiliated by Nehru'. Looking lost and vaguely troubled, he added, 'The basic reason could lie in the two-nation theory that led to Partition. But you must never overlook the fact that the Kashmiris are a very sentimental people and the ill treatment meted out to their hero Sheikh Abdullah did leave an impact. Of course, later other issues came into play. I do not like to comment on the day-to-day happenings these days, but I would like to stress that repression does not and cannot help change the minds of the people.'

At least in this view Qasim has been consistent. In a feature published in *Sunday Mail*, the columnist A.G. Noorani wrote:

> ... the rigging of the election to the State Assembly in March 1987 has been universally censured. So repressive was the policy of the Rajiv Gandhi government that Mir Qasim was provoked to say on 24 April 1989: 'This government has to decide what it wants, the people of Kashmir or just the land ...'

When I reminded Qasim of this observation, he looked pained. His only response was that he was not in favour of independence for Kashmir. 'For the simple reason that Kashmir cannot actually remain independent for long ... there's China, there's Pakistan.'

Sceptical of politicians and political activists, I have always put greater store by what dispassionate observers have to say about Kashmir. Journalists aren't always at the top of my alternative list, but there are a few exceptions, chief among them being Ajit Bhattacharjea, Director of the Press Institute of India, whose book *The Wounded Valley* stands out among the several books written in the last decade on Kashmir. He has no political agenda, and he did not write the book sitting in an air-conditioned room in New Delhi after a short trip to Srinagar. He was witness to the events in Kashmir in 1947–48, and has travelled through the Valley on numerous occasions since. I remember meeting him on polling day during the 2002 elections in a village in the south of the Valley. There were heated exchanges taking place between the security men, the agitated villagers and the National Conference candidate at the polling booth and none of us journalists would risk going up to the scene of the action. But Bhattacharjea was right there, in the midst of the commotion, listening with immense attention.

When I spoke to him, Bhattacharjea was also of the opinion that the turning point vis-à-vis the unrest could be traced back to 1953. 'The Kashmiris began resenting the policies of the Government of India after that and Pakistan began to exploit the situation. Things worsened in the later years as the Kashmiris realized that the promises being made to them were not being implemented and possibly never would be—promises like the governor of Kashmir being appointed by the legislative assembly and not sent by the Indian government ... and many other such grievances. And when the situation finally erupted in 1989, the handling was so rough that people were alienated. It is the Government of India that is responsible for this alienation ... you can imagine the way the situation was handled by the fact that shots were fired even when Mirwaiz's body was being taken for burial.'

The incident he was referring to had taken place in 1990,

by which time the Valley was already in turmoil. On 21 May 1990, Mirwaiz Maulvi Farooq, the religious head of Muslims in the Valley, was shot dead at his residence. When his coffin was being carried in a procession, the Central Reserve Police Force (CRPF) opened fire on the mourners, killing twenty-four of them. 'It's been pretty rough handling by GOI,' said Bhattacharjea, and with incidents like these as examples, it is difficult not to agree with him.

Two passages from Bhattacharjea's book, read together, show how little and yet how much has changed in the India–Kashmir equation from 1947, when Indian troops went into Kashmir to drive out foreign invaders, to the early 1990s, when the troops came back to beat down the Kashmiris themselves.

Of what he witnessed in 1947–48, Bhattacharjea writes:

On the last day of the month [October 1947] a friend, a pilot in a private airline, invited me to accompany him on a flight to Srinagar ... the Dakota flew low and Kashmir unrolled slowly before us with a graduated deliberateness not available in the jet age. Only when we circled to land at Srinagar could we see that all was not well in paradise. Columns of smoke were rising from the villages beyond. We landed on the dirt airstrip to find several other aircraft already there, unloading men and their weapons. The raiders, we were informed, had been pushed back five miles from the outskirts of the airfield which they had threatened to seize three days earlier. Troops were still being ferried directly to the front. Bearded men, unmistakably Muslim, who in Delhi would have been regarded with suspicion as possible agents of Pakistan, were gathered around the buses and trucks that lined the approach to the airfield. They were the men who ferried the troops ... and when we hopped into a jeep [for a] ride into the city, we found volunteer groups, organized by the National Conference, patrolling the roads and guarding the bridges. The Maharaja's police had fled with him. Even so, many shops were open and traffic was moving. There was no question of insecurity. The people around us ... mostly Muslims but with many Hindus and Sikhs among them ...

I was posted in Srinagar in the summer of 1948, when the Pakistan army was openly engaged in war. By then the threat to Srinagar had receded, for the enemy had been pushed back to the edges of the valley ... There were no security guards for Sheikh Abdullah ... He travelled in a single car with Begum Abdullah and the writer. He was welcomed in every village. Not every Kashmiri may have supported the National Conference, but disagreement never extended to violence within the valley ... But when I suggested to New Delhi on the basis of this experience that Kashmiris were unlikely to vote for Pakistan in a referendum, few believed me. The distrust of Muslims, magnified by partition, was too deep. Over the years, tension with Pakistan and communal politics in India drove this doubt deeper, enhancing reverse doubts in Kashmir. Yet diplomatic observers, at least in [the] early years, did not share Indian doubts. US State Department files reveal that Chester Bowles, US ambassador in the early fifties, cabled Washington on 16 November 1951, that he had asked all chiefs of diplomatic missions in New Delhi as to who would win a plebiscite in Kashmir. Their response: each without exception stated that India would win; margin varied from three to two to four to one ...

And of the scene in 1993, he writes, with rare forthrightness:

Landing in Srinagar in May 1993 was like entering hostile territory ... No bearded locals, except for one or two policemen, were visible at the airport. Everyone was frisked and the place was ringed with paramilitary troops, their automatic guns at the ready. The road into town was

studded with sandbagged bunkers with light machine guns
poking out from slits. It was patrolled by soldiers in jeeps
and squads on the road with fingers always near the
triggers. In town, the familiar road to Jhelum Bund was
interrupted by security force encampments; entry into
several stretches was prohibited, the club was the Central
Reserve Police headquarters ... the row of houseboats on
the Dal were empty; so were the shikaras ... Hotels on the
lakeside boulevard were occupied by security forces.
Government officials were ferried to and from the secretariat
in guarded convoys ... Politicians were noticeable by their
absence. They were on the militant hit list ... everyone
was willing to talk ... Antagonism was targeted on the
security forces and the government behind them. Almost
everyone I met wanted azadi ... They or their families had
fallen foul of the security forces; they were all full of stories
of torture and repression, horrifying even if one-tenth was
true; and some were.

*

Perhaps one in ten million Indians outside the Kashmir Valley
has any doubts about India's absolute right to Kashmir; so
we are casually tolerant of the military operations in the state.
There are many who believe that the Kashmir issue remains
unresolved only because India is a 'soft state'. It is the kind
of conviction that results from near total ignorance of history.
The peace activist Sushobha Barve drew my attention to this
aspect recently: 'Tell me, why don't we tell our people the
simple facts? How many Indians are aware of the historical
facts vis-à-vis Kashmir? Most of us don't even know that
while the rest of the country was engaged in the independence
struggle against the British, Kashmiris were fighting on another
front altogether—their fight against the Dogras.'
Successive Indian governments have not bothered to make

public the facts about Kashmir's accession to India and its special status in the Union. This is clearly not a sin of omission. If the problem in Kashmir is now out of hand, these governments must take the blame. Any negotiated settlement—the only kind possible—will involve a degree of compromise. But by continuing to encourage the vast majority of its citizens to view the entire issue only in stridently nationalist terms, as a battle between Pakistani militants and the Indian army, the Indian state may well be closing the door on that possibility.

Any government serious about dealing with the Kashmir dispute will have to begin by making ordinary Indians understand that Jammu and Kashmir was always a special case; it is the only state in the Indian Union where two Constitutions are followed, and there are sound historical reasons for this. To quote from Justice A.S. Anand's book *The Constitution of Jammu and Kashmir*:

> When the partition of India came, Kashmir was in a state of political unrest, the public demand for a Constitution was the result of a number of grievances. The autocracy of the ruler, the denial of fundamental rights, his anti-Muslim policies and the inefficiency of his government kept the public in a state of discontent ... [J&K] forms a part of the territory of the Indian Union but its constitution does not form a part of the Constitution of India. It has its own constitution enacted by its own constituent assembly and as it was framed by the representatives of its people, it was tested at every stage to ensure its suitability to the people concerned ... To understand the development of the constitution of J&K, one has to go far back into history ...

Justice Anand also points out that the history of the region cannot be fully understood unless we realize the significance of Kashmir's geographical position that made it the favourite of invaders and refugees, and also for its strategic importance to every major empire in the subcontinent, from the Mughals to the Sikhs and the British.

*

The twelfth-century text *Rajatarangini* by Kalhana mentions Gonanda I as the earliest ruler of Kashmir and dates his reign as approximately twenty years before the Mahabharata war. The next prominent ruler Kalhana writes about in detail is Emperor Ashoka, who ruled Kashmir through a deputy who had a seat of government at Taxila. Ashoka is believed to have introduced Buddhism in Kashmir and built the original town of Srinagar—known as Srinagari then. His dynasty was followed by the Kushana dynasty, the Huns, the Karkotas and the Loharas. Hindu rule in Kashmir terminated with the close of the reign of Raja Sahadeva.

The spread of Islam in Kashmir was largely due to the Sufis, who sought refuge here from the upheavals in Central Asia in the early fourteenth century. The graves of these Sufis dot the landscape of the Valley, and the influence of Central Asian traditions is apparent even today. Many of my Kashmiri friends maintain they have family trees tracing their ancestry to Central Asian countries. For the nineteenth-century traveller Colonel Torrens, a walk through the 'suburbs of Sreenuggur' was 'enough to induce a relapse into … dreamy memories of Stamboul'. (Some historians and travellers like Sir Walter Lawrence and Sir Francis Younghusband, interestingly, have commented on the Jewish features of the Kashmiris and concluded that Kashmiris are one of the lost tribes of Israel—not a view that Kashmiris would welcome today! (Farooq Abdullah, whose popularity had already nosedived in the mid-1980s and has remained at rock bottom since, has also been attacked by his detractors for his Jewish connection—his son-in-law being Jewish.)

The spread of Islam continued under the Sultans and the Chaks. It was from the Chaks that the Mughals took Kashmir in 1586. Mughal rule in Kashmir lasted for 166 years and left a strong influence. The contribution of the Mughals in administration, architecture, the laying of gardens and roads in this region is well known, but few know of the pragmatism and sensitivity that informed their policies in the region. Akbar, for instance, had directed his military commander to fix the camp for his army away from Srinagar, at the foot of Hari Parbat, to keep the soldiers in one place and under check so that the day-to-day life of civilians would not be disturbed. Dara Shikoh, Aurangzeb's brother, set up the first ever school of Sufism in this part of the subcontinent. Called Pari Mahal, its ruins still stand not far from the Chashme Shahi. Aurangzeb himself proved his pragmatism when the Jami Masjid (Srinagar's main mosque where the Friday prayers are held by the Mirwaiz) was completely gutted in a fire that also destroyed the chinars growing in the Masjid's compound. The much maligned emperor is believed to have said that a masjid could be rebuilt but the loss of the trees was much more serious since it took a chinar one thousand years to reach its full height.

Perhaps it was the distinct culture of Kashmir that inspired these rulers to conduct themselves sensibly. Few regions in the subcontinent have been home to so many seers and poets. Through the various stages of religious change, from Vedic Hinduism to Buddhism to Islam, Kashmiris absorbed the most appealing aspects of spirituality. The synthesis of mystical Shaivism and Sufism resulted in Muslims revering Lalleshwari as Lalla Arifa and Hindus adopting Sheikh Nooruddin, the patron saint of the Valley, as Nand Rishi. 'Kashmiriyat', a common, shared cultural tradition—including rituals performed at the time of birth, marriage and death, and also language, food, dress and names—that reflects a common ancestry, bound the Kashmiris of different faiths together. Only in recent years, since the late 1980s, have religious exclusivists and fundamentalists among both Hindus and Muslims begun to question and undermine this shared heritage.

Perhaps Kashmiriyat survived as long as it did because of frequent and long periods of tyrannical rule by outsiders in Kashmir, beginning with the Afghans in 1752. Every Kashmiri was persecuted—even if one community, depending on the faith of the tyrant, suffered a little less at times than the other—and this kept the communities together, a bond born of shared loss, grief and humiliation. Of the Afghans, the historian G.M.D. Sufi writes in *Kashir*, his two-volume history of Kashmir:

> The Afghans signalized their stay by roughness and harshness. Their chief victims were ... the bold Chaks and the brave Bambas as also the Shias. The Sunnis did not fare better. It is said of the Afghans that they thought no more of cutting off heads than of plucking flowers.

The Sikhs who followed (1819–46) the Afghans outdid them as oppressors. William Moorcroft, who was in Kashmir in 1824, records:

> The Sikhs seem to look upon the Kashmiris as little better than cattle. The murder of a native by a Sikh is punished by a fine to the government of sixteen to twenty rupees, of which four are paid to the family of the deceased if a Hindu and two rupees if he was a Mohammedan.

And the traveller Baron Schonberg, who visited Kashmir during the latter part of the Sikh rule, went as far as to say, 'I have been in many lands but nowhere did the condition of the human being present a more saddening spectacle than in Kashmir.'

The Dogras, who ruled from 1846 till Partition, came to be the most hated of Kashmir's rulers. To ordinary Kashmiris, especially the Muslims who constituted the majority of the population, they were 'zulm parast', worshippers of tyranny. Muslims were discriminated against in every walk of life: if the Dogras ever needed to employ a Kashmiri in the state administration or the armed forces, he had to be a Hindu. During Dogra rule, only Hindus had the benefits of education; the Muslims remained landless peasants and craftsmen. Sir Walter Lawrence records:

> When I first came to Kashmir in 1889, I found the people sullen, desperate and suspicious ... they were forced by soldiers to plough and sow and the same soldiers attended at harvest time. They were dragged away from their homes to carry loads to Gilgit. Every official had a right to their labour and property. Their position was infinitely worse than that of the *tiers etat* before the French revolution.

The Dogras had acquired Kashmir from the British, through a treaty that is widely regarded as perhaps one of the three most significant turning points in Kashmir's history. Till 1846, Jammu, Kashmir, and Ladakh were separate areas under different rulers. Jammu was ruled by the Dogra chieftain Gulab Singh, who had been appointed raja of the state by Maharaja Ranjit Singh, of whose Sikh empire Jammu was a part. Gulab Singh later conquered Ladakh and added it to his territory. Kashmir came to him through a war that he stayed out of, and an outright sale. In November 1845, six years after the death of Ranjit Singh, war broke out between the Sikhs and the British. The Sikh nobles asked Gulab Singh to help and lead them, but he chose to remain neutral. After the war, the victorious British rewarded Gulab Singh by appointing him prime minister of the Punjab. The British government also demanded of the Sikhs a war indemnity of rupees one and a half crore, fully aware that they were not in a position to pay so much. The plan was to get the Sikh Darbar to offer 'Cashmere' instead of the payment and transfer it to Gulab Singh in exchange for a compensation. As Lord Hardinge put it, 'A Rajput state independent of the Sikhs on the right flank of our Beas frontier would strengthen us and weaken the Sikhs, and this I consider most desirable.' On 16 March 1846, a treaty was concluded between Gulab Singh and the British government by which Kashmir was made over 'for ever and in independent possession to Maharaja Gulab Singh and male heirs of his body'. The compensation Gulab Singh paid the British government—for an area 84,471 square miles and two and a half million people—was rupees seventy-five lakhs.

As rulers to whom the Kashmiris had, literally, been sold, the Dogras naturally did not start off as the favourites of the people. They, of course, made it worse by making discrimination on the basis of religion an instrument of state policy. The alienation of the Muslims reached its height during the rule of Hari Singh, who ascended to the throne in 1925. The noted Kashmiri intellectual Pandit Prem Nath Bazaz, quoted by Justice A.S. Anand in his book, was unsparing in his report on the condition of the Muslims under Hari Singh:

With Hari Singh's pro-Dogra policy in operation, the people of Jammu, particularly the Rajputs, got most of the jobs while the pandits were recruited as clerks in offices vacated by the Punjabis. Needless to say Muslims were as yet out of the picture. The degree of communal discrimination was revealed by the fact that even now under the State's Arms Act, only Rajputs and Dogras were permitted to own and use firearms. Non-Dogras were not given any chance to serve in the army till 1930.

Justice Anand also quotes Sir Albion Banerjee, the prime minister of Kashmir till 1929 when he resigned because of the policies of the maharaja:

> Jammu and Kashmir State is labouring under many disadvantages, with a large Mohammedan population absolutely illiterate, labouring under poverty and very low economic conditions of living in the villages and practically governed like dumb driven cattle. There is no touch between the government and the people, no suitable opportunity for representing grievances ... the administration has at present little or no sympathy with the people's wants and grievances.

This was the state of affairs in the 1930s when Sheikh Abdullah, among the few educated young Kashmiri Muslim activists at the time, emerged as a political leader opposed to the maharaja's repressive rule. In 1932, with Mirwaiz Yusuf Shah, he formed the All Jammu and Kashmir Muslim Conference, which later became the National Conference after Abdullah and Shah parted ways. Secular in his outlook, a brilliant orator, Sheikh Abdullah, once revered as 'Sher-e-Kashmir' or the Lion of Kashmir, was to lead the struggle against Dogra rule and was later instrumental in bringing Jammu and Kashmir to India. It is important to point out that the instrument of Kashmir's accession to India, which was signed on 27 October 1947 by Maharaja Hari Singh, also needed to be endorsed by the leader of the main political party in Kashmir—Sheikh Abdullah of the National Conference. Otherwise, chaos would have resulted, given that the Muslim-majority state was ruled by an unpopular Hindu ruler. Sheikh Abdullah did endorse it. But supporters of Sheikh Abdullah claim that he gave his consent in view of the strange and completely unexpected turn of events when armed Afghan intruders from across the border stormed Kashmir. At that time, they say, Abdullah had no choice; he had to safeguard the people of the Valley. He agreed to Indian help in repelling the invaders, not to the accession.

In an interview Justice Anand told me, 'Where's the confusion? Sheikh Abdullah told the constituent assembly [as late as] 1954: "Today is the day of destiny that comes once in the lifetime of a nation. Decide what you want—India, Pakistan or independence." And the constituent assembly passed a resolution to be part of India, so where's the confusion? It's just that our public relations have been poor.'

But talk to any Kashmiri in the Valley and he not only does not agree with this but says rather blatantly and confidently that the Kashmiri was let down by both Hari Singh and Sheikh Abdullah and to an extent by Jawaharlal Nehru as well. As Prem Nath Bazaz writes in his book *Whither India After Independence*:

> Kashmir has proved the graveyard of Jawaharlal Nehru's professions and ideals. In a huff he decided in 1947 to accept the accession offer of the almost deposed maharaja without referring the matter to the verdict of the state's people. Ever since, he had to add one injustice to another to stick to that unfair and undemocratic decision ...

Ajit Bhattacharjea dwells on the complexity of the accession when he writes in his book that the only point on which Sheikh Abdullah and Hari Singh ever agreed was that they would have preferred Kashmir to be independent. Barely a month after the accession, Abdullah apparently said that 'it would be a very good thing if India and Pakistan were made to recognize the state as an independent unit like Switzerland', and the maharaja nodded his assent. The maharaja's motive, says Bhattacharjea, was to preserve his dynasty; Abdullah's to protect his people. In his letter of accession, Hari Singh had clearly restricted New Delhi's role to just three areas: external affairs, defence, and communications. Later, he even considered withdrawing accession. When Nehru took the Kashmir dispute to the UN, following the invasion by Afghan raiders, Hari Singh wrote to Patel, complaining that he was ignored in India's reference to the Security Council even though Kashmir's accession could not have been legalized without him. 'Sometimes I feel,' he wrote, 'I should withdraw the accession that I have made to the Indian union.'

Sheikh Abdullah, too, continued to look for ways to secure Jammu and Kashmir's independence despite the accession that he agreed to. He met diplomats of various missions and, while in New York in 1948, met Warren Austin, the US representative at the UN, who wrote to the US Secretary of State George Marshall:

It is possible that [the] principal purpose of Abdullah's visit was to make it clear to [the] US that there is a third alternative, namely independence. He seems overly anxious to get this point across ... he did not want his people torn by dissension between Pakistan and India.

Abdullah, from available evidence, remained an India loyalist despite his dismissal and arrest in 1953, but he clearly kept looking for a way to fulfil the 'need for self-determination

... an inherent right of all people'.

So there was little difference in Hari Singh's and Sheikh Abdullah's ideas on independence for Kashmir. But nobody ever charged Hari Singh with being anti-national, while Abdullah, who made the more courageous choice in endorsing the accession to India, was branded a traitor, a Pakistani agent, and imprisoned. It is indicative of what exactly has been wrong with India's attitude towards Kashmir all along.

The refusal to acknowledge the complex nature of the accession is born of the same attitude. The basic facts that we are never told about are these: Technically, when Hari Singh was forced to seek India's help to repel the invaders, in exchange for signing the instrument of accession, the princely state of Jammu and Kashmir was an independent state after the withdrawal of British paramountcy. When the instrument of accession was to be signed, the Governor General of India, Lord Mountbatten, introduced a clause to provide for the rights of the Kashmiri people. In his letter of acceptance, dated 27 October 1947, he says:

> Consistent with their policy that when the issue of accession has been the subject of dispute the question of accession should be decided in accordance with the wishes of the people of the state, it is my government's wish that as soon as law and order have been restored in Kashmir and her soil cleared of the raider, the question of the State's accession should be settled by reference to the people.

So the British did leave a loophole in 1948 itself.

Also, in the same year, on 20 February, India had agreed to a plebiscite in Junagadh, a princely state with a majority Hindu population but a Muslim ruler. The plebiscite went in favour of India. India's position today would have been far stronger if it had asked for a plebiscite in Kashmir as well.

Many believe that in 1948 people in this Muslim-majority state were favourably inclined towards India and had a referendum been held then, they would have opted for India. It was only later that the mood soured.

Several factors have contributed to this—the absence of men like Mahatma Gandhi, confused signals coming from the Centre, an inability to trust Kashmiri Muslims, erosion of the state's autonomy, the rise of communal politics in recent years, and of course bad governance by the Kashmiri politicians themselves. Of all these, interference by the Centre in Kashmir's democratic institutions over the years has been the biggest cause. Even an enlightened leader like Nehru, said to have been passionate about Kashmir and committed to the ideal of a secular democracy, was less than fair. His handling of the Kashmir situation and his dealings with Sheikh Abdullah were riddled with controversy and a certain degree of high-handedness.

Now, of course, no transparency remains on the question of Kashmir. Ordinary Indians and Pakistanis know none of the truths about the Kashmir situation post-1947. Robert G. Wirsing writes in his book *India, Pakistan and the Kashmir Dispute*:

> One reason for this is that public access to official Indian, Pakistani and Kashmiri archival materials relating to this phase have been largely choked off by the governments of India and Pakistan ... In this phase major decisions about Kashmir were in Indian and Pakistani hands; the British documentary record for this period while instructive is much less revealing.

Now that over half a century has passed, it is unlikely the whole truth will ever be known. No Pakistani government can be expected to make records public; and the present right-wing government in India is more unlikely than even the previous ones to do so. And for neither country is it now possible to let Kashmir go. Mountbatten's clause in the accession document, the UN's suggestion for the withdrawal of Pakistani troops from POK and referendum in all of Kashmir—all these are no longer relevant. For India, particularly, complete independence for Kashmir could well mean disaster—not just in the context of the Indian Muslims but also the North-East and other states with insurgencies. Of course, there remains the option of maximum autonomy— and India, at least, would benefit by turning itself into a genuinely federal state—but this most workable solution has no supporters in the establishment.

*

The present generation of Kashmiris do not talk much of the sale of Kashmir to Gulab Singh, the Dogra rule or even the events of 1947–48 and the injustice meted out to Sheikh Abdullah (indeed, things have changed so much that the grave of the Sher-e-Kashmir now needs to be guarded round the clock). Most of them are aware of these historical facts but they are not of immediate consequence to them. What they talk about is the blatant rigging of the 1987 elections, soon after which Kashmir came to a boil.

The events leading up to the 1987 elections are themselves illustrative of how the Indian government bungled things in Kashmir. In 1981, four years after perhaps Jammu and Kashmir's first free and fair elections had brought Sheikh Abdullah back to power, the Sheikh nominated his son Farooq as his political heir. The Sheikh died in 1982; Farooq became chief minister, and nine months later led the National Conference to another victory in the state. Relations soon soured between Mrs Gandhi's Congress, in power at the Centre, and Farooq Abdullah. The reason for the serious differences, according to some, was Mrs Gandhi's insecurity and her dictatorial ways. There are others who maintain that much of the fault was Farooq's—he was politically inexperienced and made a habit of grandstanding. Looking back now, it seems to have been a bit of both. The result was that Farooq Abdullah's government was dismissed and Jagmohan—at one time Mrs Gandhi's staunchest loyalist and now an equally loyal supporter of the BJP—was appointed governor. Farooq Abdullah was furious, he was hurt, and in his inimitable fashion he let the people of Kashmir know that he was.

Incredibly, by 1986 Farooq had formed an alliance with the same Congress, now led by Mrs Gandhi's son and political heir, Rajiv. Not surprisingly, the alliance lost him considerable support among the people of Kashmir; those who weren't angered and disgusted by the turnaround were confused. When elections were announced in 1987 it was widely believed that the National Conference–Congress alliance wasn't going to have the easiest of times. But Farooq Abdullah defied the prophets of doom and returned to power. There were allegations of massive rigging, charges that Farooq dismissed, as did the Congress, but hardly anyone was convinced.

The people of Kashmir felt betrayed, and Farooq, by discrediting himself and his party through his alliance with the Congress, had proved to them that they could hope for nothing from Indian democracy or from any pro-India political party of the state like the National Conference. I quote a page, dated 25 March 1987, from the private journal of a Kashmiri friend:

The inevitable has happened. Farooq Abdullah has returned with greater strength, arrogance, defiant and proud in his treachery. This is the age of base pragmatism, cold arithmetic, of narrow personal interests and the relentless pursuit of power and luxury, of blind hero-worship and the propagation of the cults that the dead heroes of cowardly and weak and ignorant people generate ... This was expected, but one hoped against hope that providence in its benevolence would set right the wrongs done, at least to those innocent and gullible Kashmiris whose only fault was that they loved their land and also loved freedom and human dignity ... one wonders if the final epitaph is being written on the death of Kashmir this day—25 March 1987 ... but you cannot bury history like you bury people, even those people who make and unmake history ... History is nothing if not a balancing act of nature. It takes its own path and tends to swing the course of life the other way when one extreme is needed ... [it is] the valiant who shall inherit the earth ... as it is not in the nature of the pragmatists, the cowardly and the miserly of heart to do so. It is always the valiant who mould history—history shall be remade only by the valiant, again and again.

The 'valiant' were everywhere in the Kashmir Valley in the months following that infamous election. By late 1988, anti-India protests had become frequent, as had police firings that resulted in casualties, and bomb and grenade attacks by militants. In 1989, Rubaiya Sayeed, daughter of Mufti Mohammad Sayeed, then the home minister in the barely one-month-old V.P. Singh government at the Centre, was kidnapped by the JKLF. She was released in exchange for five JKLF leaders who were in jail. Their release on 13 December was celebrated by huge, cheering crowds in the streets of Srinagar. In the days that followed, more people were killed in police firing and curfew was imposed. Things were spinning out of control for the Central government, and V.P. Singh reacted by bringing back Jagmohan—hardly the most popular man in Kashmir after his first stint in 1984—as governor, at which point Farooq Abdullah resigned.

In the autumn of 2002, as I went probing into the reasons that led to this eruption, politicians in the Valley minced no words. Muzaffar Hussain Baigh, a senior minister in the present Congress–PDP government, said, 'Even Constitution-abiding citizens like Salauddin and Yasin Malik and my junior colleagues turned anti-state once they saw that great injustice ... the blatant rigging in the 1987 elections.' And Mehbooba Mufti, PDP's vice-president, said that there had been no proof of Pakistan's interference till after those rigged elections, which was also the view of the once dreaded militant Baba Badr who entered into an understanding with the Government of India in 1996. 'You take up the gun only in the final stage,' he said, sitting across the table from me in the restaurant of Hotel Broadway. He said it so gently, a boyish smile on his frail face, that it was hard to imagine him with a gun.

He took to the gun in 1983, he said. 'I'd failed in class ten, dropped out of school and joined Shabir Shah's organization, People's League. In the initial stages I was in charge of holding protests and it was easy to motivate the youth towards our ideology. It was in '87 we started looking for contacts in Pakistan to train our men. At the time, developments in Europe—the fall of the Berlin Wall, the disintegration of Russia—and the ongoing jihad in Afghanistan, the revolution in Iran, all these held out some hope about the unification of both the parts of Kashmir. In 1989, Naeem Khan and I entered Pakistan via the LOC—yes, by foot, and it wasn't easy. We had to reach there to arrange for Shabir Shah's visit to Pakistan, it was important, but he was arrested at Rambhan and then it was decided that I stay put in Pakistan. Nothing was very clear, but the mood was to get rid of India ... Anyway, I got back to India in January 1990 and formed the Muslim Jaan Baaz Force [an outfit of Shah's People's League], which became the largest organization after Hizbul Mujahideen, with a membership of three thousand men. But I was arrested soon afterwards, in '91, and kept in solitary confinement for thirteen months.'

He paused at this point and I expected to hear about his experience in prison, but he said nothing of that. Instead, he talked about his disillusionment with Pakistan. 'It was while in jail in Srinagar that I introspected. Lots of time to think clearly, there wasn't much else to do. And soon after my release I went back to Pakistan to find out the missing links that had been bothering me. It didn't take me long to see the folly, the futility of it all, because I realized that Pakistan had political and diplomatic interests which had little to do with our Kashmiri cause.'

In fact, today, more Kashmiris than at any time in the recent past seem to be aware of the politics of the region and realize that Pakistan is in no position to provide them with stability. In 2001, during the time I was travelling through the Valley, the focus was on Parvez Musharraf's visit to India and most Kashmiris were glued to the TV. One academic, Dr Abdul Majid Baba of Kashmir University, had even begun work on a book on the 'Vajpayee–Musharraf Agra Summit'. Yet they were all cynical. They shook their heads in dismay and made mutterings to the effect that it would, as one man put it, be a 'kathbaath' affair—one of them would eat and the other would talk and that would be the end of the circus. 'Nobody will know what ails us, what our problems are, because nobody listens to the apolitical here. Your New Delhi ministers only listen to the likes of Farooq Abdullah, who like his dead father says one thing to us and something entirely different to them. He had won in the earlier elections by abusing the RSS men and now he's one of them!' the man said, referring to Farooq's alliance with the BJP at the Centre. 'He betrays us and yet he has the licence to talk on our behalf!'

When I asked them about Musharraf and Pakistan, they were clear that it was not merger with Pakistan that they wanted but a 'kind of independence'. When I pointed out that some Hurriyat leaders were openly pro-Pakistan, they shrugged and said that it was sheer politics at play. The only emotional link they had was with POK, for obvious reasons.

The younger Kashmiris hold pretty much the same views, but their cynicism is expressed as a confident defiance. The confidence comes from a sound knowledge of their history, the extent of which, even among teenage residents of the Valley, often surprises outside observers. I remember a perplexed-looking Dinesh Sharma, originally from Rajasthan and posted at Srinagar's Doordarshan Kendra, telling me, 'When I point out to my Kashmiri colleagues the futility of their fight for azadi, they tell me about the historical facts—they have these on the tips of their fingers—and then all my arguments fail!'

But it isn't just India or Pakistan that the ordinary Kashmiris distrust; they have no faith in their mainstream politicians and bureaucrats either. A vast majority of the people I spoke to saw Farooq Abdullah as an opportunist. His National Conference had little credibility, and politicians in general were seen as unimaginably corrupt. For some years now, similar things are being said about the separatist leaders as well. (Corruption has always been rampant in Kashmir, but it has been more blatant in recent years. During my last visit, a contact asked me point-blank, 'What will you give me?' When I shook my head and expressed my outrage, he continued, completely unfazed, that he had done nothing unusual.) The apathy, the corruption, the decay of the administrative system are all the result of a long period of bad governance, but the situation has worsened over the last decade and a half, ever since Kashmir became a state under siege. If sending in the army was seen as some sort of solution to a crisis, the cure has turned out to be far worse than the illness. No government can win over a people by converting almost their entire state into a military camp. The manner in which the army has conducted itself in Kashmir—or been asked to by successive regimes in New Delhi—is often not very different from how it would function in hostile foreign territory. Perhaps this is only to be expected; it is not the business of the Indian army to fight wars within India's borders, among people we consider fellow Indians, but that is exactly what it has been charged with doing in Kashmir, every single day since 1990.

That sending in the army, in the manner that it was, was a mistake became clear almost at the very beginning. I go back to the record I kept of my visits to the Valley in 1990. I checked into the vacant Hotel Broadway in Srinagar on 25 May that year, and could not sleep the first few nights. There was an eerie silence on account of the curfew, broken only by sounds of gunfire and almost regular cries from not so distant quarters. In the mornings there would be people, many in tears, talking openly about the human rights violations that had taken place the night before. I was the only woman occupant of the hotel, which anyway had only a handful of people staying in it—of the 103 rooms only ten were occupied and the 350-strong staff had been cut down to sixty-one. Talk of cops in plain clothes moving in the corridors of the hotel added to the tension. One morning I spotted a middle-aged Sikh whom I was certain I had met somewhere in New

Delhi. Not familiar then with the games of governance, I went up to him, trying to chat and find out the details of the turbulence, but of course he wouldn't talk beyond the brief, short sentence that was in itself a strange sort of greeting. I dismissed him as an arrogant babu, but was later told that he was an Intelligence Bureau man. I saw him again in New Delhi, on more than a few occasions, but he would always pretend that we had never crossed each other's paths in the corridor of that hotel.

I never got used to the sudden bursts of gunfire and the human cries. The third or fourth night, I developed a vicious headache and asked the hotel staff for some medicine but they showed me an empty medicine kit, and of course there was no question of anyone going out to find a twenty-four-hour chemist. Even if he did, said one of the waiters, a young man, I remember, who used to cycle all the way from Pampore every other day, there would be no point in it; none of the shops would be open. He sat and made me a herbal paste, using spices from the hotel kitchen, which I rubbed on my forehead. It worked, but not for long, for almost at the crack of dawn, J.M. Qureshi, the advisor to the then governor, Jagmohan, dropped in to meet me with about twelve pairs of uniformed legs following him. The sight of so many policemen was unsettling enough, and then the interview itself proved so frustrating that my headache returned. Qureshi was a wall, and gave me nothing beyond the denials and completely useless and unintelligent official one-liners. When I confronted him with instances of confirmed rape and molestation, he dismissed them as mere 'dhakka mukka' (push and shove) cases. 'Our men have to break into some homes, so they have to push around,' he said, that was all there was to it. When I pressed him, asked why it was necessary to push around at all, was there a 'hard policy' being followed, he replied, 'Can't comment on hard policy.'

Later, in an interview with Jagmohan himself, I encountered the same callousness. The entire stretch leading to the governor's house was so full of security bandobasts—complete with grim-faced security men aiming their guns directly at any visitor—that it made a mockery of the message that the governor had read out to the people of the state after his second appointment in January 1990:

> ... the current phase should not be called a period of governor's rule but a period of governor's service. Constitutionally, I would be a governor, but for all practical purposes I would function like an orderly—a nursing orderly—to help the patient, with love, compassion and service, to regain his health, become vigorous and vibrant and lead a life of peace and productivity.

Who would dare walk that long, formidable stretch to voice his or her genuine grievances to this 'nursing orderly'? I asked the governor. He responded with a look of injured innocence, something that I discovered was typical of him (he was to later write a book about his Kashmir years, titled, bafflingly, *My Frozen Turbulence*, giving his version of events). People did come to meet him, he insisted, there was no problem. If I was interested, I could be shown photographs to prove this. When I later mentioned this during a conversation with Bahauddin Faruqi, he explained that those photos being put on display were all taken during Jagmohan's previous stint as a governor.

Jagmohan, for all his convoluted, wearying and often obfuscatory talk about compassion and nursing orderlies, had made up his mind to be tough. Given his track record, especially during Indira and Sanjay Gandhi's Emergency regime in the mid-1970s, it is not surprising that he went overboard. That he appointed two former police officers as his advisors was only a small indication of how he intended to go about the business of governing the Valley. Though I must add that one of the two advisors, Ved Marwah, who had been the Delhi police chief, had the reputation of being a fair and efficient officer—a 'soft cop'. But he couldn't really do much about the tough policy being relentlessly followed by the governor. The two times I dropped into his office during that time, first to collect my curfew pass and then to have it extended, I remember him looking harassed and tense. Marwah and others like him would certainly have wished they were elsewhere through Jagmohan's five-month tenure in 1990, when much went wrong, and terribly so.

The day after Jagmohan assumed office, close to 100 people were killed when the police opened fire on a crowd of protestors at the Gaw Kadal Bridge. In March, shortly after the director of Srinagar Doordarshan, Lassa Koul, was murdered by militants, Kashmiri Pandits left the Valley in large numbers, encouraged, many believe, by Jagmohan. That created a communal divide where none existed till then. Over the next two months the situation deteriorated further—more protests, more civilians killed in police firing. Through those months, journalists, both Indian and foreign, reported on the havoc Jagmohan's policies were wreaking on the lives of ordinary Kashmiris and the damage they were doing to India's image. Going back to those reports, the year 1990 seems to me the year of the written forewarnings that were never heeded.

Citing observations made by an eight-member joint committee of four leading human rights organizations of India, the *Hindustan Times* reported on 28 April 1990 that 'the "tough" policy adopted by Jammu and Kashmir governor Jagmohan has not only proved counterproductive but has further alienated the people of Kashmir ... [who] have been virtually driven to the terrorists' fold due to hatred generated by the repressive measures of the state administration'. In the *Times of India* of 13 May 1990, veteran journalist Nikhil Chakravarty wrote: 'It is possible for the armed forces at the disposal of the government of India to overpower the armed secessionists not numbering more than 5,000. But how do we win over the 35 lakh Kashmiris who inhabit the picturesque valley?' The government, he wrote, was preoccupied with the immediate job of silencing the secessionist's gun and nothing else seemed to matter, and that 'the police action may itself destroy to a large extent whatever attachment or goodwill the people in the Valley may have towards India beyond the Banihal'.

The most moving account of everyday life in the Valley that I remember from the time is Ayesha Kagal's in the 'Sunday Review' (*The Times of India*) of 29 April 1990:

Today, truth flips faces somewhere in the middle of the Jawahar Tunnel, the two-and-a-half-km-long leaking lifeline that connects, or divides, depending on how you view it, the valley from the rest of the country. Two separate realities exist on either side of the tunnel, two entirely different sets of perceptions. And two terrible stereotypes congeal to face each other. To the rest of India—exposed to an unrelieved diet of militant kidnappings, killings, bomb blasts and Pakistan's forays, together with the BJP-abetted pandit problem—the face of the Kashmiri is now dissolving into a blurred featureless mask. He has become a secessionist-cum-terrorist-cum fundamentalist traitor. An image exemplified in the April 30 *India Today* cover and its story. In Kashmir, on the other hand, the face of India crystallizing into focus is that of a weapon-wielding oppressor, a *darinda*, a beast, not human ...

'... each day in Srinagar, a hundred rumours bloom, circulate, fade and are reborn .... Television, then, is seen as an utterly one-sided government mouthpiece and to even the brief visitor to the valley the yawning discrepancy between Doordarshan's views from New Delhi and the ground-level reality in Kashmir is evident. The governor's New Delhi utterances that there are no shortages may convince the rest of the country. It's a little more difficult to do so in a lower-middle-class home where the children have had no milk for eight days, where the son has been foraging the slopes of the Shankaracharya hill for edible shrubs because there are no vegetables and the family has subsisted on rice and dal for the last ten days ...

This is the month of Ramzan, the month of rozas, fasting, where from dawn to dusk a 14-hour long abstinence is offset by the evening meal of good nourishing food. Iftar, the breaking of the fast, is usually done with dates, milk or fruit, followed by the main meal of rice and meat dishes ... This year, iftar was usually observed with water, and dal was the staple in practically every Kashmiri Muslim household .... We define ourselves in many ways, food is one of them. Religion another. And this year in Kashmir, curfew put paid to a number of Muslim festivals .... Huddled in a corner of his downtown home, past a maze of narrow streets flanked by open drains, a retired government employee cradles his kangri, more for comfort than warmth and, speaking almost to himself, recites a verse by Akbar Allahabadi: *raquibon ne rapat likhwai / ja ja ke thanon mein / ke Akbar naam leta hai / khuda ka iss zamane mein* [my adversaries have lodged reports / with the police, of my crime / that Akbar is taking the name / of the Lord in these times ...]

The international press too carried reports of the horrific results of the crackdown. India had rarely come across in such bad light. Tony Allen Mills's report in the *Independent*

(London) of 28 January 1990 quoted an eyewitness who 'talked about the point-blank firing on a crowd by the CRPF ... shots, shots and shots ... if they saw movement, a leg or a hand or a head, they would fire again and again. They were saying: "So you want Pakistan, you want independence...?"' For William Dalrymple (in *Sunday Times*), entering Kashmir was 'like flying into an army base ... unarmed, the Kashmiris have faced the machine guns of the third biggest army in the world'. In *Time Magazine* (5 February 1990), Edward W. Desmond wrote: 'Like a mad fury, the will to protest—at any cost—swept through the wintry Kashmir valley ... at least 133 people were killed last week, all but nine of them civilians.' And David Housego's 15 May 1990 report in the *Financial Times* stated quite bluntly that 'India's democratic traditions have suffered the damage that comes from using force to cow a segment of its own people'.

No one in charge of our Kashmir policy seemed to have read these reports or else they convinced themselves that these were either fiction or the propaganda of bleeding-heart activists, whom it was as fashionable to ridicule and hate then as it is today.

Jagmohan's worst critic was the trade union leader H.N. Wanchoo, who was later gunned down, on 5 December 1992, by unknown killers. Often, this frail man would drop in to meet me at the Hotel Broadway. We would sit by the lawns of the hotel, and he would shriek his disgust at Jagmohan's policies. Sometimes I tried to tell him to be discreet for the sake of our safety, his and mine, and he would shrug and say even more loudly, 'It's plain repression here ... the BJP and RSS lobbies have openly said that Jagmohan has been sent by them ... There's no clear government policy on Kashmir— the National Conference and Congress people have run away, the Opposition has closed down, warrants have been issued against the moderates, political activists are banned, so with whom will the government talk! Today, Mufti [the Union home minister at the time], George [then minister for Kashmir Affairs], the PM [V.P. Singh] and the governor say different things. Mufti had said in Jammu that Hindus would be sent back but the very next day Jagmohan had their ration cards in Jammu extended till September 30 ... Today, press notes are prepared at the Raj Bhavan and from there they go directly to Doordarshan and AIR. Facts are being hushed up— yesterday an entire marriage party was shot dead, but you wouldn't have heard this, of course, because this news was not allowed to circulate.' For every visit, Wanchoo came armed with details of all the excesses being committed in and around Srinagar; he had the casualty list for almost every single day.

My own days were spent visiting hospitals. It was the only practical thing to do, for one could actually see the numbers of those injured in firings and shoot-outs. There were also the large numbers whose nerves couldn't cope with the situation, and Srinagar's lone government hospital for psychiatric diseases (it is still the only one) seemed to be overflowing with patients, many of them lying in the central court and the open corridors. Seventy-year-old Gul Mohammad, a retired director of the statistics and planning department, who was among the many patients I met at another hospital in the city, haunts me still. He could not believe that the very government he had served for so many years couldn't be bothered with the injuries inflicted on his body and his psyche. 'I live in the Amira Kadal locality and at about 11.30 a.m. it seemed as if all the bunkers of the city began raining shells on the area ... soldiers burst into my house, fired shots in every direction ... nobody knows how many of us are alive and in what state ... Why did they shoot at me ... what's happening here ...' he kept asking me helplessly.

Doctors seemed as disturbed and helpless, barely able to cope with the rising numbers of the dead and injured being brought in. Cutting across religious lines, they all expressed their anger at the government's repressive policy. Most of the wounded they treated had head, neck and chest injuries, they said, suggesting that the security forces were firing high, violating the most basic rule of policing civil unrest. This to me was further evidence of the danger of sending army men, trained for years to bring down enemy soldiers, to manage internal unrest. (And in Kashmir, of course, it was also assumed that the local police, with a majority of Muslims in its ranks, could not be trusted.)

'Criminal acts of the worst form are going on because of the curfew imposed by Jagmohan,' Justice Bahauddin was to say to me in May, the month Jagmohan finally resigned. 'The records of a leading hospital show the intake of 22,992 patients between December 1988 and June 1989. But now, December 1989 to May 1990, the intake is only 8661. This means that 14,000 people couldn't get to the hospital because of the curfew. Of those who do [manage to reach a hospital], records at SMHS Hospital show that five or six patients injured in the crossfire have been admitted there every day, and since Srinagar has seven other hospitals you can imagine the numbers of those injured in crossfire alone!'

It seemed to get worse at night. One night, fear got the better of me and I telephoned the *Times of India* correspondent Askari Zaidi to ask whether I should shift out to some other, smaller guest house, but he said that there was no reason to fear. So I stayed, trying to shut out the sounds of a kind of war at night, and even the horror tales recounted to me during the day. When I could, during the brief hours that the curfew was lifted, I would walk through Lal Chowk, towards the Bund and take the ferry across, trying to pretend things were normal again. But in the ferry too there were people with stories to tell, and fellow journalists looking worn out and depressed. After one ferry ride, depressed and worn out myself, I met Yousef Jameel, working for the BBC then and now with *Asian Age*, at his home which was close to the Bund. He was nursing a swollen eyelid. 'I've been bitten by a Pak-sponsored spider,' he said sarcastically. I asked him how bad things really were, given the official line that things were being brought under control by Jagmohan. 'If you say the problem is over or under control, you'll be deceiving yourself,' he said. 'True, there are anti-India sentiments, but Jagmohan's repressive measures can do little to bring about any solution, in fact they are turning more and more youth anti-India. The militants say they are ready to talk, provided GOI agrees to implement the UN Resolution and if there is an international guarantee too. But GOI says that talks are possible only within the Constitution. So the problem will continue.'

And it has.

Nineteen ninety was the year when you could see the beginning of a revolution, no one could miss it. (Though several older Kashmiris will correct you and insist, perhaps a little romantically, that it began after they and other young men at the time saw *Lion of the Desert*, the 1980 film about the Arab hero Omar Mukhtar, who fought the Italians in Libya during World War II.) Jagmohan resigned as governor in May 1990, to be replaced by a former RAW chief, Girish Chandra Saxena. That the head of the country's top intelligence outfit had been appointed to govern them was the worst kind of signal to send the Kashmiri people. In any case, by this time things had pretty much spun out of control.

The violence grew and spread to areas outside the Valley in the state. In addition, militant groups backed by Pakistan, like the Hizbul Mujahideen and later the Jaish-e-Mohammed, became active in J&K. Allegations of human rights violations by the security forces fighting these groups now became routine. There is a piece, written by Sukhmani Singh for the *Illustrated Weekly of India* of 30 September 1990, that I still retain, for it encapsulates the tragedy of that year. I reproduce a part of Sukhmani's report below:

> .... These are the bitter angry outbursts of Kashmiri women who have been sexually assaulted. Ironically enough by the keepers of law and order—the Indian army and the security forces stationed in the valley since January this year to curb the growing terrorist menace. Today the sight of a man in uniform both infuriates and frightens them. While the villages in the interiors have witnessed the highest number of rapes, those close to civilization have not been spared either ... Three unmarried sisters from a well-respected family in Lal Bazar, a downtown area of Srinagar, were carried off to the cantonment and released after two nights of sexual assault. More than anywhere else the number of atrocities have reached alarming proportions in army-infested Kupwara, a thickly forested mountainous district 90 kilometres north of Srinagar, earlier famed only for the beauty of its Lolab Valley ...

Sukhmani Singh then goes on to give details of each of the victims, whom she tracked down and who spoke to her voluntarily. It is a courageous piece of investigative journalism, and a harrowing one that I still find savagely depressing. The only comfort I have derived from it is that there is at least such exemplary evidence of a free press that I can use to defend our democratic traditions when I am told that Indian democracy is in fact a sham. Though of course it has to be said—and this has particular relevance to the Kashmir problem—that had such a report appeared today, when simplistic right-wing propaganda has become official policy, Sukhmani would have been labelled anti-national.

*

So whatever happened to the revolution? I recall a conversation with a taxi driver taking me from the airport to the Hotel Broadway in May 1990. No sooner had I used the term 'militant' in a certain context than he turned around and with a piercing look in his eyes said sharply, 'Our boys are not militants, they are mujahideens [revolutionary heroes] ... don't use New Delhi language in this place.' Today you hire a cab or an auto or hop into a bus and you could call militants by any name and no one will be provoked to angrily defend them. But there will be many there who, if they feel they can trust you, will tell you that militancy in its true spirit has spread out, anger and resentment simmer in the hearts of all Kashmiris. As the Mirwaiz of the Valley told me, 'With all its might GOI has not been able to crush the sentiments of the people and our struggle is on ... there could be just three to four thousand militants in the Valley but that's not what is important, for every Kashmiri wants a solution to this ongoing struggle of ours. You could call it a slow revolution; we are fighting for freedom from a system where there is no accountability, where no one is sure who is working for whom.'

A majority of the Kashmiris point out that the struggle continues; it has only changed complexion. The BBC's Srinagar correspondent, Altaf Hussain, who also happens to be from the Valley, told me, 'According to me the complexion of the turmoil has changed—it has become like guerrilla warfare, assuming a definite pattern, and the focus has shifted from the towns to the interior. Also, today more youth are turning anti-establishment than in the past years, so much so that last May [2001] at Moulvi Farooq's death anniversary I was surprised to see that more than ninety-five per cent of the crowds comprised very young people.'

No one familiar with life in the Valley believes that the worst is over. People haven't forgotten the recent past; their faces go grim when they talk of the bloody encounters they witnessed in the early 1990s. Even politicians who participated in the 2002 elections confide that 'elections are okay not just for civic problems ... [they are more important] for keeping alive the chances of a dialogue with the Centre'. Mehbooba Mufti was more than categorical when she said that elections are no solution, for the real issue remains unsolved even now. In an interview with me soon after the 2002 elections, she seemed to say the same thing more diplomatically: 'I agree that no election can resolve the Kashmir problem but the newly elected representatives can play the important role of facilitators in the peace process.'

In the early 1990s I would often be nudged by my companions who would excitedly point out adolescent boys, with what seemed like guns clutched firmly under their phirans, walking hurriedly past us. Today you will rarely see such sights. But to presume that young men have all realized that militancy is not an option would be a mistake. Masood Rahi, a freelance photographer, said to me, 'All of us have had our share of being roughed up by the security forces, or worse. So you see, in fact, it is difficult to be sure who *isn't* a militant! The movement is on. Maybe discreetly, but it is on.'

Many young Kashmiris, however, are also a bit cynical

about the older militant leaders. They talk of the 'money pouring in from agencies within the country and from outside', money that they say goes into the pockets of some of those who first gave the movement a fillip. When asked for names, though, nobody goes beyond the Abdullahs. Even if Omar Abdullah, Farooq Abdullah's suave son and the new leader of the National Conference, is given a clean chit, the rest of the family, including his wife, are not. And if one asks about the Hurriyat leaders, there is an initial silence, followed invariably by arguments in their favour. Once, during the course of an interview in 2002 with Naeem Khan, the present head of the National Front who was among the first to spearhead a students' movement—the Students League—and was later arrested along with Shabir Shah in 1989, I decided to stop beating about the bush and ask directly if he personally or any Hurriyat leader he knew had been lured. 'Definitely, agencies are at work to try and cause divisions,' he said, '… *unki bahut koshish rahi hai*—they tried hard to cause divisions through various means, but I don't know of any Hurriyat leader who has received money.'

'How is it that they live in bungalows and drive about in fancy cars?' I asked.

'This is all part of the propaganda against them,' he retorted. 'If some of them drive Sumos, why is that unusual? After all, owning a car isn't such a big deal today—you get them on easy loans.'

Others are quick to point out that there are leaders who live very simply—like Yasin Malik, who lives in rather cramped conditions in his ancestral home in the congested Maisuma locality of Srinagar. Who pays for his heavy medical bills and foreign trips, then, I ask. He has had three recent surgeries in USA that would have cost a minor fortune. They tell me that the surgeons who attended to him were all of

Indian origin and didn't charge a penny, that he stayed with friends, and as for the rest of the expense, it was borne by the Kashmiri groups in the UK and the USA.

Yet, there are hardly any charismatic, universally popular leaders now as there were in the late 1980s and early 1990s. So while the disaffection and resentment remains, you will see little of it on the surface since the movement has no visible face. Perhaps this is more worrying, for hatred and anger festering in young minds cannot be good news for the future.

Communities: Old Harmonies, New Divisions

I have never been made more conscious of my religious identity than during conversations with some fellow journalists or friends before a trip to Kashmir. 'You're Muslim,' they say, 'you'll be safe, but we ....' The ease with which people say this sort of thing is surprising, considering that Kashmir has no history of communal strife. During Partition, when tens of thousands were being massacred in the name of religion in much of north India, not a single incident of murder, rape or arson was reported from Kashmir. Speaking of more recent times, the JNU academician Kamal Mitra Chenoy, who, as a human rights activist, moves about freely all over the Valley, affirmed that he has never felt threatened. 'You'd be shot dead only if the militant bodies suspect you to be a government informer. I have never had a problem, never felt insecure ... there's nothing anti-Hindu.'

There is a misconception that only a handful of non-Muslims—unless they are human rights activists or journalists—visit the Kashmir Valley these days. There are, in fact, several of them in Srinagar at any given time, and not just tourists but people who work there. The well-to-do normally tend to restrict themselves to 'secure' hotels like the Grand Palace, but I've seen many Hindus working as sales agents in the shops in the Polo View market and on Residency Road, going about their business just as ordinary Kashmiris would. There are also professionals like Rajeev Bhalla, an employee of Rail India Technical and Economic Services Ltd (RITES) posted in Srinagar as part of the team working on the Qazigund to Baramulla railway line, who was staying at the same guest house as me in late 2002. He was in charge of testing the soil and rock capacity along the entire stretch, from Katra to Qazigund, since the line has to pass through seventy tunnels. Bhalla was anything but low-profile— boisterous, gregarious, fond of butter-chicken and paranthas. Anyone could tell that he was a Punjabi, and, given his name and the fact that he wasn't a Sikh, it was also apparent that he was a Hindu. I asked him how his family reacted to his being posted in Kashmir and moving around so freely. 'In the beginning, my wife was paranoid,' Bhalla revealed. 'But this summer I asked her to come down from New Delhi and took her all over the city. Though she wore saris and bindis, there was no problem at all, and then she was relieved.'

His boss, Surinder Madan, also a Hindu from outside Kashmir, had tried the same approach with his wife and it had worked. Still, for the sake of abundant caution in a disturbed region, they hadn't quite struck up friendships with the local people—especially the Muslims—which was not surprising, considering what Indians outside Kashmir get to hear about the connection between Pakistan, the jehadis and the Kashmiris (read Muslims). And yet, something interesting happened one evening in the dining hall of the guest house. I had barely entered when Bhalla rushed in from the lawns, shouting angrily: 'There's another story waiting for you— the cook [a Muslim] has just returned and he says that his son was beaten by the security forces at their village in some place called Tanmarg ...!' Soon, he was joined by the aged cook and while the cook wept, Bhalla told me the details: the man's young son had been picked up by the army, beaten and released only after the newly elected PDP MLA Ghulam Hassan Mir intervened. The waiters and other staff members also crowded around, each giving fresh details and narrating other incidents of the high-handedness of the security forces in rural Kashmir. Bhalla's agitated, high-pitched voice could be heard above everybody else's through all this, and every once in a while he turned to the weeping cook to console him. Nothing, for me, could have been greater proof than Bhalla's words and actions that evening that neither he nor his colleagues had experienced any communal violence, threats or prejudice in Kashmir. He was not a human rights activist, or a journalist; he was a sensitive human being bonding with another. I wonder what the chances would be of such a scene being played out in any other part of the country.

If Bhalla's story seems too dramatic an example, here's another. For some years now, Niraj Seth of the Rajiv Gandhi Foundation (now working with ActionAid India) has been visiting the remotest villages of the Valley as part of the Foundation's work with adults and children in distress. In all these years the question of her faith came up just once. A village elder asked her, '*Beta, tum kya musalman ho*? [Are you a Muslim, my daughter?]' And when she replied in the negative, there was no reaction; nothing changed in her equation with the people of that village and she was never asked the question again. Niraj is categorical: 'It's wrong to say there is a religious or communal problem there.'

But present-day politics has worked overtime to dent this perception. Attempts to create a communal divide in Jammu and Kashmir are not new, but they have become more blatant during the BJP-led NDA regime. Today, the average Indian isn't ready to believe that Kashmir is not another Gujarat, with the Muslim as aggressor. He will not believe that there are still several thousand Pandits living in the Valley, as there are Sikhs and Christians, none of whom have had to change their names, remove their nameplates or dress differently. And of course he has never been told that the majority of the dreaded renegades (militants who surrender and are used by the security forces) and the state-government controlled Special Task Force personnel who did the dirty work for the previous state government are primarily Muslims.

'Why do the right-wing forces insist on giving a communal slant to the Kashmir crisis?' asks Mirwaiz Umar Farooq, the religious head of the Valley Muslims and a former chairman of the Hurriyat Conference. 'The Kashmir issue is not about Hindus and Muslims; it is made out to be a religious issue by vested communal interests. Why can't people be told that there's a political problem here, definitely not a religious one.' Indeed, almost all Kashmiri leaders—separatist or otherwise— insist that religion is not a factor in the Kashmir dispute as they see it. They do not hesitate to say that they are little concerned with the disaster that might erupt for Muslims in the rest of the country if Kashmir does get independence. The Indian Muslims were given a choice in 1947, they reason, and if they chose to stay in India and not move to the Land of the Pure, then India is their country, it is the country of their choice. In fact, Hurriyat's senior leader Professor Abdul Gani Bhat even went a step further in his rationale in the course of my interview with him at his Wazir Bagh set-up. 'You say that there could be chances of Indian Muslims getting massacred if we get freedom, but weren't they anyway massacred this year [2002] in Gujarat?' What he was implying, in effect, was what the activist and lawyer Parvez Imroz said to me more clearly: 'We Kashmiris can't be held hostage because of Indian Muslims.'

This remark is interesting, for there is a tendency among non-Muslims to see all Indian Muslims as a homogenous mass. The fact is that the Kashmiri Muslim has always seen himself as separate from and superior to his co-religionists in other parts of India. And the Valley Muslims are indeed different from Muslims in the rest of the country. Even the casual observer will see the difference, most notably in the architecture.

The ziarats and dargahs in Kashmir are built in a distinctive version of the Indo-Saracenic style. The peaked pyramidal roofs, instead of the domes seen elsewhere, resemble the pagodas of the Far East. These pyramids have a square base corresponding with the general squareness of the building. The outer roofs are invariably tiered and painted green and the walls are white. The ceilings are mostly khatamband, a specialty in Kashmiri woodwork that consists of thin panels of pine wood pieced together into geometrical designs. Similar ceilings are said to be found in Algiers, Morocco and Istanbul. (The historian and author Percy Brown, in fact, has pointed out architectural similarities with the wooden churches—stavekirks—of Norway, built between the eleventh and fourteenth centuries.) Another striking difference, apart from the architecture of the shrines, is that while in dargahs in the rest of India there is a tradition of very openly asking for donations, in Kashmir there are boxes kept for donations and no one will pester you to donate.

These are only the obvious signs that you will see on the surface. You get a better sense of the difference when you interact with the local people. When in Kashmir, I have often felt conscious of my identity as a Muslim from UP. On several occasions there have been subtle remarks and gestures that made it clear to me that to the Kashmiris I am a Muslim of 'inferior stock'. I remember walking into the Pir Sahib mosque situated opposite the UN office on Gupkar Road one afternoon to offer juma namaaz, and the ladies assembled in the women's segment of the mosque looked at me with faint contempt; they were quiet, but their looks said, 'Where in hell has this dark-skinned, clumsily clad outsider descended from?' Kashmiri friends who accompanied me to certain downtown areas were amused to see me tie my dupatta rather too earnestly round my head and throw a shawl around my shoulders. 'Do what you want,' they'd laugh, 'but you will always stand out as a non-Kashmiri!'

A tolerant, gentle Sufi Islam has been the dominant faith in the Kashmir Valley for centuries. Since the mid-1990s this has been threatened by the regressive, orthodox interpretations of Islam that the mostly foreign jehadis have brought into the Valley. Thankfully, at least for now, all that is attractive about the Muslim faith in Kashmir holds out against the jehadi mentality. Though, of course, for an 'inferior-stock' Muslim like me the pride of the Valley Muslim can sometimes be trying! I felt a kind of relief each time I met a non-Kashmiri Muslim in the Valley—Ziauddin, the young blanket seller from Sitapur whom I met in Kupwara, the Mirwaiz's personal secretary Syed Rahman Shams (who had earlier served Umar's father), the several Urdu-speaking government employees (not all Muslims) who had been transported there from Uttar Pradesh for the polls, or the bhaiyya cooks at the eating joints serving non-Kashmiri food in Srinagar's main shopping area. I suppose it is a special chemistry that works between people who share a native place. Syed Rahman Shams couldn't get me an appointment with the young Mirwaiz (after two appointments were cancelled at the last minute, it was a single telephone call to Sheeba, the Mirwaiz's wife, that brought success), but he helped in a very special way—by making me feel not so alone in Kashmir. He talked excitedly in Urdu, telling me how long it had taken him to be accepted by the locals in Srinagar—despite having been brought personally from Deoband at the age of seventeen by the former Mirwaiz. Things were beginning to improve gradually, and then the senior Mirwaiz—Mirwaiz Maulvi Farooq—was gunned down by unknown assassins on 21 May 1990, and he was back to square one, an 'outsider'. 'Integration' finally happened only after the present Mirwaiz retained him as personal secretary and, more importantly perhaps, after he married a Kashmiri from a downtown family in 1992.

Kashmiris themselves, especially the Muslims, rarely marry outside the Valley, which, given the dim view they have of non-Kashmiris, is not surprising. Through the later half of the 1990s, though, this had begun to change a little, with the turbulence in the Valley forcing parents to seek grooms for their daughters in UP, Bihar, Delhi and other states. But the young seem to be putting their foot down now. Several university students I spoke to had strong views on the subject: no, they would oppose being married off to outsiders; they could only relate to a Kashmiri, they said, because only a Kashmiri could understand their situation—what they had endured and why, how their day-to-day life was a struggle. There were two rather glamorous-looking sisters, daughters of a Kashmir cadre bureaucrat, in one group of students I met, and they were the most categorical of the lot: 'We will only marry a Muslim—otherwise according to Islam it is no marriage. And he has to be a Kashmiri, no question about it.'

*

A valley ringed by high mountains, Kashmir developed a distinct culture that sets a Kashmiri apart from not just the people of other Indian states but also of Jammu and Ladakh.

Within the Valley, Kashmiriyat—shared customs and language—has bound the different religious communities, especially the Muslims and the Pandits, for centuries. Several 'outsiders' living in the Valley have said to me, 'You must see two Kashmiris talking—whether a Pandit or a Muslim—how they go on gossiping in Kashmiri, ignoring us completely ... worse than Bongs, or even the French!' I can think of numerous occasions when shopkeepers would look at me and my non-Kashmiri friends and with wry smiles playing on their lean faces, mutter words that made them laugh and giggle while we busied ourselves examining shawls or tomatoes, trying to mask the fact that we felt stupid and self-conscious. Even as a journalist I have had to brave such typically Kashmiri moments. Accompanying Ehsan Fazili of the *Tribune* and UNI's Aurangzeb Naqshbandi to cover the re-polling in Kupwara in 2002, I endured their constant chatter in Kashmiri all through the drive, and their guffaws and cackles as they cracked 'Sogami jokes' (Sogami was a well-known politician of yesteryears from the Lolab Valley, remembered to this day for his utterances and also his flab— but this I found out later). Once in a while they would notice me and apologize casually: 'Sorry, but these things can best be talked about only in our lingo.'

It was a coincidence that Ehsan and Aurangzeb were both Kashmiri Muslims. It would be the same even if one of them had been a Pandit, or even a Sikh. Only a couple of weeks before that drive to Kupwara, I had travelled with a group of photojournalists to Shopian and Anantnag and had to keep asking them to translate their jokes into Hindustani for me. The same afternoon, at a lunch hosted by the then director of information, I had sat sandwiched between two boisterous Kashmiris, Amit Wanchoo of *Al-Safa* and Tariq Bhat of *The Week*, who gossiped non-stop in Kashmiri. Even their gestures matched! At the end of it Amit looked at me, noticed my discomfort and irritation and by way of an apology, said, 'It's our language, you know. It's the Kashmiri language that has kept us Pandits and Muslims together.'

Today, it could be said that the shared language wasn't enough. Nor were the common food, customs, songs, even the saints. For, if they were, what would explain the mass exodus of the Pandits from the Valley in 1990? Today there are no clear figures of the exact number of Pandits still living in the Valley—Kumar Wanchoo (the forty-eight-year-old son of H.N. Wanchoo) with great confidence put the figure at 'over 18,000', but Siddharth Varadarajan in a report in the *Times of India* (1 September 2003) wrote that 'thirteen years after the Kashmir violence began, the Pandit community in the Valley is on the verge of extinction'. He used figures from a survey by the Hindu Welfare Society Kashmir (HWSK) which found only 8865 Pandits left in the Valley, spread across 270 villages and mohallas. Whatever the exact figure, it is a fact that a majority of the Kashmiri Pandits now live outside the Valley, many still in refugee camps or cramped quarters. Of those who remain in Kashmir, most prefer a degree of anonymity, except for a few like the retired Lieutenant Colonel S.K. Dhar, Vijay Dhar and the Wanchoo family.

Those of both the Muslim and the Hindu right with an interest in Kashmir cite the flight of the Pandits as an example to conclude that Kashmiriyat was always a façade, a strange sort of beast conjured up by liberal non-believers. But there has always been a debate about that exodus: was it a natural migration, or was it in some way engineered? Interestingly, even many well-known Pandits, who refused to be part of that exodus, blame the then governor Jagmohan, now a BJP minister, for encouraging it. During the autumn of 2002, while I was in Srinagar, I witnessed an argument between a commissioner-level officer and Lieutenant Colonel S.K. Dhar. The bureaucrat was trying to equate the post-Godhra massacre of Muslims in Modi's Gujarat with the exodus of the Pandits from the Valley. But in seconds he was rebuffed. 'Let me put it this way,' said Dhar, 'if instead of encouraging the Pandits to leave, Jagmohan had encouraged them to stay, many wouldn't have gone from here. If the situation really *was* beyond his control, shouldn't he have resigned and gone back to New Delhi instead of continuing to sit here as governor?' In the People's Union for Civil Liberty (PUCL) report released in April 1990, several activist bodies had clearly blamed the establishment for that tragic turn of events. To quote from the report:

> Regarding the exodus of Hindus and Sikhs from the Valley, the committee members are of the strong belief that the Muslims genuinely want them to come back. Not even a single case of arson or looting of non-Muslim property has been reported so far ... the migration of non-Muslims to Jammu [from the Valley] started after some vested interests propagated that they would be provided with free plots there.

No one knows if this is entirely true, but a significant number of the Pandits who were part of that exodus did return of their own accord a few years later.

H.N. Wanchoo had spoken along the same lines, and would still have been doing so, I'm sure, had he not been murdered—a murder still unsolved—in 1992. Ten years later, I decided to find out whether his family had changed their minds about the issue since. It wasn't difficult to locate them, for they are a well-known family of Pandits who to this day continue to live in Srinagar's Jawahar Nagar. I met Kumar Wanchoo, who runs a pharmaceutical business and also finds time to work for the APDP. He seemed more than confident about staying back. 'In fact, even after my father was killed I didn't move from here because he was against the exodus, and so moving away from here would've meant moving away from the very purpose of his mission. It's not just my immediate family but my four sisters and their families too who are still in the Valley. There are more than 18,000 Pandits here, we have our welfare associations and every Sunday we meet at Ganpatyar to take stock of the situation. The reason we have managed to stay here and live in peace is because 90 per cent of the population has no communal tendency whatsoever. Jagmohan was clearly playing a role for the Government of India. I must tell you that when I interact with the Pandits who fled to Jammu, they realize their mistake, they see the complete futility of the exercise.'

The Hurriyat leaders stress that Pandits should have no reason to fear—the late Abdul Ghani Lone spoke about this for several minutes when I interviewed him in the summer of 2001, when he was under house arrest. 'I am against any bifurcation talks, against division of the state on any religious lines. This state belongs to all of us Kashmiris—whether Buddhist or Pandit or Muslim. You are asking me why the Pandits left—we didn't want them to go, *un becharon ko jaana pada*, they had to leave because the then governor instilled a sense of fear in them.' Two years later, his son Bilal said the same thing: 'Foremost, it is important to have an investigation into who encouraged them to go. I strongly feel that they have every right to be here as honourable citizens, this is what the Quran teaches.' JKLF's Yasin Malik has often said that he feels 'incomplete without the Pandits'. 'They have to come back home,' he told me in an interview. 'They were not driven out by us; they were encouraged to leave this place by vested political interests. Kashmir has never faced a communal situation, even during Partition when the communal factor was at its peak in the rest of the country there was peace here because of our secular character. Mahatma Gandhi had himself commented on this.'

Other Hurriyat leaders voice the same opinion. But the fact remains that a number of Pandits were gunned down in the 1990s. Today, the average Kashmiri Hindu does not feel optimistic; he is confused about the future. Many Pandits wonder what their fate would be if Kashmir does become an independent nation some day, or if the state is trifurcated or even bifurcated along religious lines. Where would they go then? And what if riots were to follow any independence or the division? Some even worry about a backlash in their Muslim-majority home if there is a repeat of the Gujarat experiment in some other state. It is true that the Pandits in the Valley do not live in the kind of fear that the Muslims of Gujarat do. But a majority of them feel insecure. Most of the Hindu women I met at the Residency shopping complex were bold enough to go about in saris, wearing large red bindis on the forehead, but when I asked them for comments on the situation in the Valley, or even asked for their names, they refused to talk. Some of the non-Muslim staff of the Hotel Broadway said that though their families had decided not to move to Jammu, they weren't entirely comfortable, nor did they feel completely secure. The Amla brothers, who run the hotel, are from a prominent and wealthy Hindu family of Srinagar. They are the sons of J&K's Congress treasurer Krishna Amla and grandsons of Tirath Ram Amla, the most successful businessman of the Valley who came to Srinagar from Muzaffarabad in 1931 and settled here. Even they confessed to feeling insecure, and added that business wasn't picking up either—so the family was investing in the hotel and restaurant business in Delhi. The fact that the brothers continue to visit Srinagar regularly and continue to run their hotel and other businesses there is remarkable, considering that the 1990s were particularly trying times for the family— the Broadway theatre was burnt down, in all probability by the militants, and the Hotel Broadway was taken over by militants for eight long years.

Krishna Amla's sister, too, continues to live in Srinagar. Kiran and her husband Vijay Dhar did shift to Delhi in 1990, but returned within a couple of years. They maintain one of the finest homes on Srinagar's upmarket Gupkar Road, and in contrast to the Amlas, are investing in a future in the Valley, not outside: they have set up a branch of the prestigious Delhi Public School on a nine-acre stretch of family land at Athwajan. Vijay Dhar drove me to the site, where the building was ready, well in time for the first academic session that was to begin a few months hence, in March 2003. For most people, such a venture in today's Kashmir would appear an extremely unusual, perhaps even foolhardy enterprise. I asked Dhar about this: didn't the turbulence and uncertainty about the region's future bother him? 'Many factors were responsible for our decision,' he explained. 'The most obvious one is the fact that today this state has the lowest literacy rate in the country. Do you know that the CBSE system [one of the two standard systems of education that apply in schools through much of India] is not followed here? When I went to the CBSE headquarters in New Delhi to get them to grant permission for this school, a junior officer had the cheek to ask me whether I was a Muslim or a Pandit! Such is the thinking these days. I feel very, very strongly for this place, for the people. Today, the Kashmiri is socially and economically insecure. He is in a dilemma, caught between the security forces and the militant groups. And then there's the frozen mindset of New Delhi—the priorities of the government seem lopsided. No one seems to understand that all that the Kashmiri wants is to live in peace, in dignity.' During the course of that conversation, Vijay Dhar had also said, quite matter-of-factly, 'I face no problem living here.' I had no reason to doubt that, despite the fact that he had a personal security officer—that was more likely a necessity because of his wealth rather than his religion.

That evening at his house I met Kiran, whom I couldn't help but admire for her quiet strength, and her father, Tirath Ram Amla. Ninety-year-old Amla was sitting next to his wife Satya, born deaf and mute, whom he had married in 1939 against his family's wishes. Amla was happiest talking about his early years of struggle, before his business began to flourish, and when I interrupted to get his views on the state's recent history—which had directly affected his business as well—he looked glum. After a silence he mumbled, 'In my autobiography I'll be writing about all this. The common man is affected by the security forces, but then India cannot afford to give up Kashmir. We have already fought two wars on Kashmir ... maybe there'll be another, because Pakistan seems equally determined.' Did he face any problems now as a Hindu? Absolutely none, he said, which was why he continued to stay in Srinagar, moving to New Delhi only for a few months when winter was at its peak.

It is important to point out that not all non-Muslims feel this way. Delhi-based filmmaker Arun Kaul, a Pandit, had left the Valley some years before the 1990 exodus. He went back on regular visits, though, and had even built a new home for himself in posh Barzullah. Sometime during the turmoil of the early 1990s, however, it was looted and partially burnt. 'By the neighbours,' he replied quietly when I asked him who was responsible, and went on to give me details of what had been stolen. Even the electrical fittings had been ripped out and taken away. To this day you can see gutted bungalows that are clear signs that at least in the 1990s things weren't going too well for the minority communities in Kashmir.

I remember cruising down the Dal Lake in a motorboat along with a couple of other journalists. Rumours about regular custodial deaths were rife at the time, and jehadi terrorists from Afghanistan and Pakistan had entered the Valley too, and as we went past Chinar Bagh, the Gaw Kadal gate and Amira Kadal, anxious faces peeped out of the dongas parked all along the stretch and wondered aloud if we were part of a search party looking for bodies. As if this wasn't depressing enough, we passed rows of soot-blackened shells of houses along the Habba Kadal and the large, abandoned building of the Vishwa Bharti School. All full of people once, till they left, and their homes and schools became anybody's property: looters, petty thieves and arsonists; militants in search of hideouts and army men in pursuit of the militants.

There are countless mysteries that crowd Kashmir today, among them, the reason why and how the Pandits left—whether they fled or were misled and encouraged to leave. Auto and taxi drivers are usually good sources of information, but on this issue what they told me didn't add up to any satisfactory answer. In 1990, a Hindu driver, Avtar Krishan of Chhanpora locality, had looked very disturbed when he told me that though he had an ancestral home in Srinagar, he planned to shift out to Jammu. 'It is not death per se that one is worried about; but the constant threats I keep receiving ... there's no peace of mind. And I have my family to think about. Police protection is all very well, but will we get it all our lives? I have already packed off my family and soon I will have to shift out of this city too.' Were they Muslims, the men making these threats, I asked. The question made him nervous and he refused to comment. I wish he had, because in the years that followed, almost every single driver I spoke to, whether Muslim, Hindu or Sikh, seemed rattled and unhappy like him and spoke of going elsewhere. So it seemed as if the situation in the Valley had affected every normal person who wanted nothing more than a basic security and some hope of a better future, and it remained as difficult as before to understand the particular fear or injustice that might have caused the Pandits to risk becoming refugees.

The Pandits who muster the confidence to come back to the Valley cannot bring themselves to go back to their original homes, to rebuild or restore them and start living there again. In late 2002, at the Kashmir University's department of English, as I sat waiting to interview Hameeda Bano—the senior faculty member who openly denounced the Indian army in Kashmir as an occupation force—I met an anthropologist, Professor T.N. Pandit, who had returned to the city of his birth after seventeen years. His father, in fact, had set up the English department at the university. Pandit told me that he wasn't in Srinagar on work. 'I have no work here. *Bas, aane ka dil kiya* ... I have been wanting to come back for years—this is where I did my schooling, my graduation from S.P. College.' He had an ancestral house in the city, but he wasn't staying there. Why not, I enquired. He shook his head sadly and said, 'Because our neighbour burnt it down. But you must understand, I don't blame anybody for the Pandits leaving Kashmir, nor is there any bitterness towards the Muslims. It was just that one man, our former neighbour. It was his greed. He blamed some militants for it, which is an absolute lie. No militant ever came near our home.' The betrayal was too great for him to live next to the same man again. And the government, of course, belittled his loss by offering a paltry sum of one lakh rupees as compensation.

While I spoke to Pandit, there was a woman sitting with us—introduced to me as Satya Bhama, a reader in the linguistics department—whose demeanour was quite in contrast to Pandit's, who had looked visibly troubled through our conversation, his face prematurely aged. Bhama was full of bravado but I couldn't help noticing that she was unusually self-conscious and didn't seem comfortable answering me when I asked her about her take on the situation in the Valley, particularly the problems, if any, faced by the Pandit community. There could have been any number of reasons for her behaviour, but I was struck by what another faculty member, a Muslim, said to me later. 'She's the most calculating Panditayan on the campus,' she whispered. 'She even claims that her engineer husband was kidnapped by militants. Don't believe a word of what she says.' This reminded me of similar remarks I had heard before. A certain anti-Pandit attitude, though not blatant, is discernible among urban professionals in Kashmir—or Srinagar, to be precise. Perhaps this has to do with the fact that as a highly literate community the Pandits dominate the professional services, which perhaps explains why this faint resentment is absent in the rural areas. Family temples remain intact in the orchards owned by Pandits, even where the owners have left. The Shiv mandir in Lieutenant Colonel Dhar's apple orchard is well preserved, cared for by the Kashmiri Muslim labour who work in the orchard. I was heartened by the sight of these workers rushing to meet Dhar within minutes of our arrival, and everyone sat around and chatted in Kashmiri like old friends. The man who had bought the apples for that season, I gathered, was also a Muslim.

Returning to Srinagar after a visit to the rural areas, I was more conscious of the occasions when some Kashmiri Muslim betrayed a bias against the Pandits. Seeing me walk from the

Tourist Reception Centre campus (where I was staying for the first few weeks of my visit) to the Royal Springs Golf Course with the tourism officer Anoop Kannaw, a Kashmiri Muslim was provoked to quip, 'These Pandits are such glib talkers, they manage to charm women journalists too!' What poor Kannaw had in fact been telling me was how some militants from the downtown locality had saved his family heirlooms. 'Our ancestral home is located in downtown Srinagar, and during the early days of the disturbance our ancestral collection of shawls was stolen. Months later, a militant who was known to our family came back to return them. He was in tears. He had to do this, he said, the moment he realized that the shawls belonged to my mother. She had helped his family out when they were in need and he could never forget that.'

Such bonding is still common in Srinagar. In one of the shops on Polo View, only a few days before polling began in Srinagar for the 2002 elections, I asked the man at the counter if I could make a STD call to Delhi. The man smiled and said that he wasn't the owner. 'That's Basharat Ahmad, my friend,' he said, pointing to a man outside, 'it's his shop, I'm just helping him out.' It turned out that this man minding the shop for Basharat was Ramesh Khajuria, the Panthers Party's candidate from Srinagar's Idgah constituency. Gentle-faced Khajuria was a far cry from the typical image of a politician, and he was moving about without any security. He showed me a copy of his letter to the Chief Election Commissioner asking for security, but though it was only a few days to the polls, he hadn't been provided any, despite the fact that Idgah is a very sensitive constituency, often referred to as 'Chhota [little] Pakistan'.

And yet, as far as the Valley Muslims and the Pandits are concerned, there may be no getting back to the pre-1989 ease and calm. The 1990 exodus of the Pandits has changed things subtly, as has the attitude of the present government at the Centre. There is no communal discord, but there is a new distance between the communities, especially in Srinagar. Large numbers of Pandits have been living for over a decade in cramped conditions in Jammu and Delhi, refugees in their own country. Instead of making genuine attempts to rehabilitate them, to concentrate on making it possible for them to return to the place that is their home, the government responds with grand gestures that smack of politics and mean little in concrete terms. Government employees are assured of benefits: the salaries, including retirement benefits, of all Kashmiri Pandits are intact and will be paid to them whether they are in Jammu or elsewhere in the country; there are also insurance and housing benefits. Though small cuts in the J&K Migrants Funds have already begun—the whole scheme is clearly unsustainable—it will still ensure that the migrants don't turn against the government. Meanwhile, they remain refugees, an easy vote bank, and willing supporters of right-wing agendas and suggestions to trifurcate J&K along religious lines.

In the Valley, meanwhile, people are getting used to be living without the Pandits who, being traditionally better educated, comprised the majority of the professionals—doctors, teachers, civil servants. These positions are now being filled by Muslims. Principals of some schools in the Valley I spoke to rued the fact that there aren't enough 'high quality' teachers now, and education has suffered, but things will change here too, and those who fill these jobs will clearly be an aggrieved lot if the Pandits were to return one day and deprive them of their livelihood. Some Muslims now also point out that fewer Pandits are picked up for interrogation and even fewer figure in the list of people who have disappeared. And if there is a major upheaval in the Valley, they say, the remaining Pandits can shift to Jammu or New Delhi—which are 'their cities'—but the Muslims, unwelcome outside the Valley, will have no place to escape to. It is we who suffer, they say, caught between the militant groups on one side and the security forces on the other.

Even if the changes forced upon Kashmiri society by the exodus could somehow be undone once the Pandits return, it becomes more unlikely with every passing year that they ever will. Lieutenant Colonel S.K. Dhar was candid about this: 'Most have made homes and careers outside the Valley, how can they come back after so many years? Beyond these mountains there are greater opportunities. Those who have left will find it difficult to give all that up or even to adjust in the Valley ... and to worsen conditions here, the Indian government has taken no interest in development work. Why talk of industry—you wouldn't even find cold storages in the Valley. Tell me, what would the Pandits have done here, and what can they do here even if they are brought back?'

Many from the older generation of Kashmiri Pandits outside the Valley dispute the theory that they left the Valley not out of any real fear but because it was beneficial anyway, from the material point of view, to go beyond the mountains where there were greater opportunities. They insist that insecurity made them take the crucial step of abandoning their homes. A senior Pandit confided, 'It seemed then [1990] as though Pakistan and imported maulvis had taken over the city. Loudspeakers were blaring all sorts of religious speeches with great fervour, as though Nizam-i-Mustafa would be the order of the day tomorrow. And there seemed no possibility of any police protection [for us].'

Perhaps the Pandits, being a minority, had begun to feel insecure even before 1990. There are many Kashmiri families in New Delhi who left the Valley long before the present crisis erupted. Talking to them, I got conflicting views. H.K. Kaul, whose family left Srinagar in 1965, maintains, 'It had nothing at all to do with any abnormal situation or people's attitude. We moved because we were looking for better educational and work opportunities. There was no communal problem at all—Kashmiri Muslims are among the finest people you'll meet. It's just a messed-up situation, the result of inefficiency and the Indian government's and state administration's inability to reach out to the common man. We all know into whose pockets the dole from New Delhi went—and the net result was that there were no opportunities in Kashmir. The educated youth sat without jobs and resources and Pakistan exploited the situation.' The 'messed-up situation' affected every community, according to Kaul. He maintained that even till 1989 no Kashmiri Pandit family he knew in Srinagar had any thoughts about migrating. 'In fact, in 1989, when I was visiting the city and staying with relatives in the Amira Kadal locality, we did hear gunshots at night but [my relatives] continued suggesting to me that I should buy a plot and build a house there.'

But Sudhir Dhar, a middle-class executive in his early thirties who, together with his family, shifted to Delhi just about the time when the trouble began in the Valley, disputed what Kaul had said. Even as a student in school and later in college, he had always been aware of the fact that he was from the minority community. The atmosphere was such, he said, that this was inevitable. There were others like him who told me, with no sign of agitation in their voice or demeanour, that though there was no turbulence in Kashmir before the late 1980s, sociological changes had begun to affect society around the late 1970s. 'You could see that Sufism was on the decline,' one middle-aged Pandit explained, 'and Muslims started displaying a more rigid version of Islam rather blatantly. I can't say whether politics caused this or if it was a reaction to politics, but there was definitely a change among the Valley Muslims. We continued living together like partners do in a dead marriage. You could say it was a marriage of convenience between the Pandits and the Muslims of the Valley.'

But whatever the reasons for which they left, whatever their experiences in Kashmir, the shared culture of the Valley continues to define not just the Pandits but all the Hindus or Sikhs who now live outside. Raja Jaswant Singh, the former chief justice of J&K state, who was also the chief public prosecutor in the Kashmir Conspiracy Case, was a Hindu from Mirpur, once part of undivided Jammu and Kashmir. He had been living in New Delhi for years, till his death in 2002, but the spirit of Kashmir was writ large in his everyday life: you would be offered kehwa instead of tea, the food contained generous quantities of saffron, and Kashmiris of different faiths were regular visitors to his home. One day, in what was for me the greatest proof of his true Kashmiri ethos, he extended his frail wrist towards me, asking me, a Muslim, to become his rakhi sister, despite the fact that most of his immediate family—father, mother, brother, sisters and their spouses—had been butchered in Kashmir by Afghan raiders during the invasion of Kashmir in 1947. There are at least fifty others like him whom I have met in Delhi, all defined by their Kashmiri upbringing: Jay Raina, who never misses an opportunity to charm women by reciting Urdu couplets; Rahul Jalali, who gets sentimental over a drink at the Press Club about his home, Kashmir, and tells you how even in these disturbed times he keeps going back to 'live for weeks at a stretch with friends in Srinagar'; theatre person and SAHMAT activist M.K. Raina, who never misses an opportunity to go back, even if for a few days; the artist Veer Munshi who misses authentic wazwaan feasts as much as he does his Muslim friends.

Going through a bunch of articles handed over to me recently by the former dean of the Kashmir University law faculty, Professor Shahid Siddiqi, I was struck by details of the secular character of the Valley. I quote from one of Siddiqi's pieces, written as late as the mid-1980s:

> But curiously enough there were many occasions when Kashmiri Muslims came to me and made a strong recommendation for a seat or a job for a Kashmiri Pandit. As the dean of the law faculty for many years as well as a member of the recruitment board for nationalized banks, I have been approached a number of times by many Kashmiri Muslims, recommending candidates from the other community.

It should have been so easy to preserve this harmony, but successive governments at the Centre and in the state never thought it important to do so.

If the Valley is still home, will the Pandits ever return, and work for a secure future that belongs to all Kashmiris? It seems unlikely; just as unlikely as a lasting solution to the Kashmir problem any time in the near future.

*

The Sikhs are perhaps the one minority community in Kashmir who bond with the Muslims with the greatest ease. The matter-of-fact nature of this closeness continues to amaze me, especially given the brutality of Sikh rule in Kashmir during the early nineteenth century. The apparent bonding is so strong that even incidents like the gruesome murder of thirty-six

Sikhs in Chittisinghpora in March 2000 by unknown gunmen have not created a rift between the two communities. My queries to Kashmiri Sikhs about the incident were met with words to the effect that surely I knew as well as they did that the killers were not Kashmiris. (Exactly who they were is still unclear. Within days of the massacre, the army had identified and shot down five men—all Muslims—who, it said, were the 'hardcore terrorists' responsible for the killings; but it has now been conclusively established that the men were innocent civilians.) The years of turbulence, when truth is usually the first casualty, have definitely brought about a remarkable maturity to the relationship between these two communities. While I was in Srinagar in the autumn of 2002, local newspapers had reported the rape of two minor Sikh girls. Members of both the Sikh and Muslim communities whom I spoke to were extremely worried: 'Hope this doesn't turn out to be the kind of news that will cause a rift between the Muslims and us,' said a prominent Sikh of the city. There was relief when it was discovered that the rapist was a deranged person from their own community.

In Srinagar I met a successful Sikh lawyer who was of the opinion that it was the Khalistan movement in Punjab that had inspired Kashmiris to take to the gun. *Dushman ka dushman apna dost* [My enemy's enemy is a friend]—that's still the feeling here,' he said, giving me his explanation for the remarkable rapport between the Sikhs and the Kashmiri Muslims. This lawyer had been approached by militants time and again for financial assistance, and each time, he said, he had spoken to them 'as a well-wisher should speak and made them see the futility of violence'. But at the same time, in his conversation with me he minced no words in condemning the tyranny of the boot. 'The special acts are very harsh and so there's hatred towards those in power.'

Sikhs aren't confined to Srinagar and a few surrounding villages. They can also be seen in far-flung areas of the Lolab Valley. During my visits to the interiors of the Kashmir Valley through the 1990s, I noticed fewer Pandits than turbaned Sikhs on the streets. In 1990, when anti-India protests and the government's retaliatory crackdowns were at their peak, Sikh men and women could be seen walking around in Jawahar Nagar without any kind of camouflage. During my stay in Gulmarg in 1998, the two shops I bought provisions at—the only ones that stayed open till late evening—were run by Sikhs. On my latest visits to Srinagar, in 2002, by which time I had learnt the art of 'busing' around the city, I met several Sikh passengers. 'We are Kashmiri Sikhs,' they said. Why not just Sikhs, or Indian Sikhs, I would ask. 'We are from here, from Kashmir, so Kashmiri Sikhs is what we call ourselves,' they would answer with typical Sikh confidence.

The Kashmiri Muslims recognize this, perhaps. When I met the firebrand Hameeda Bano for an interview in one of the staff rooms of the English department in Kashmir University, I noticed that she wasn't comfortable talking there because two Pandit teachers sat not far from our table. She took me to an adjoining room, where she blasted the Indian government and the security forces though a Sikh staff member sat barely two feet away. Though, at the same university, I was also made aware of the old-fashioned and perhaps practical 'thus far and no further' nature of the Muslim–Sikh bonding. Some Sikh faculty members of the Girl's College revealed that though they were absolutely at ease with Kashmiri Muslim families, marriages between members of the two communities were unheard of. One of them went on to explain: 'Love can happen. But marriage between a Sikh and a Kashmiri Muslim is impossible. *Jurrat nahin hogi* [No one would dare].'

Yet, in daily life there is such a close relationship between them that Sikhs in Kashmir talk of the situation there with as much passion, even anger, as do the Muslims. At a cyber café in Srinagar, I met a number of young Kashmiris, most of them boys, and many among them Sikhs. When I sought their views on the turmoil in their state, the Sikh boys turned out to be more vocal than their Muslim friends. Though they, too, remained clearly on guard, not entirely convinced that I was a journalist. The words of a young Sikh engineer, Pradeep Singh Balli, continue to haunt me: 'I live in Avantipoora, and the amount of blood I've seen in our locality, on our roads, has made me wary of almost everyone. I've seen people being killed at my very doorstep. Nobody knows who's who here. Like my Muslim friends I'm also affected. We Kashmiris can't trust people any more.'

*

The changes with the most far-reaching consequences, as a result of the turmoil in Kashmir, are happening not among the minorities but within the majority Muslim community. Not all these changes are immediately apparent, and not all may be irreversible, but no one who has known Kashmir before the late 1980s can fail to notice that the Kashmiri Muslim of today is in some essential manner different from what he was when there was peace in the Valley.

It becomes obvious that you are visiting a predominantly Muslim city as soon as you step out of the Srinagar airport, which is not unusual, for this has always been the case, just as any visitor to Haridwar or Amritsar can tell immediately that he is in a predominantly Hindu or Sikh city. But the difference now is that with hardly any tourists coming to the Valley, the men and women you see on the streets are all well covered in a similar fashion, complete with topis, phirans and shawls. In the past, streets were always busy and bustling, there was variety and happy commerce; now you see few happy sights. If a bandh has been declared by any of the separatist groups, the streets will be deserted. And since these days cab drivers in Srinagar rarely chat with you, you may not discover the reason for the bandh or how long it will last, till you have reached your hotel.

If you do manage to strike a rapport with the driver—and I've been lucky in this respect—he will tell you over the long drive from the airport to the city about the latest situation, the 'halaat', in the city: crackdowns, curfews, night searches, no jobs, police brutalities, fake encounters. In 2002, I arrived in the middle of a bandh—a US senator had said something foolish about the Prophet and the entire Valley seemed to be in a mood to react. In 1963, when the Holy relic disappeared from the Hazratbal Shrine, there had been violent demonstrations in the Valley, so this anger wasn't new. But I was surprised by the magnitude of the reaction I saw in Srinagar this time, given the nature of the provocation. All the local newspapers carried editorials on the subject, the Hurriyat leaders and business establishments had given a call for a complete hartal or strike and most people I met sounded bitter and upset. Discussing the issue with the BBC's Srinagar correspondent, Altaf Hussain, I asked him whether ignoring the remark wouldn't have been more mature and prudent instead of this massive protest. The man was ignorant, perhaps bigoted, living in faraway America. Why give him such importance? Altaf retorted: 'The call for a hartal is absolutely correct. It's a matter of our faith. For Kashmiris faith is a very important aspect, it is a way of life for us. It is our faith that has helped us survive the trauma and the humiliation of these years.'

This is what most Kashmiris today believe. A call for a bandh in the name of religion cannot be openly challenged in the Valley. That day in 2002 only a few private cars were on the roads, fewer buses and just a scooter or two. Of course, there was no apparent reduction in the number of government cars, which raced about with frightening speed, as usual. It took me close to an hour to find an auto-rickshaw and the driver seemed unwilling to drive. 'We are protesting against those Americans. Sorry.' He agreed only after I had explained that I was a journalist on work and wanted to see the impact of the bandh in the city. He spoke non-stop as his scooter went down Maulana Azad Road towards Lal Chowk, Jehangir Chowk and beyond. 'These Americans are after the Muslims. We support Saddam Hussain because he had the guts to stand up against US might. This time we absolutely had to go on hartal. It's a major loss for the traders because every second day there's some problem here, but with issues like these, money should not be a consideration. These American are devils—we can't even criticize their policies, but they can insult the Holy Prophet! I tell you—soon they will be here, ruling us, telling us what to do and what religion to follow. I will give up my life but I won't allow their mischief to spread here.' I was struck by his vehemence, and his arguments against America that sounded exactly like something you would hear in West Asia.

Similar sentiments were being expressed in most Muslim societies of South and South-East Asia which were also, to some extent or the other, in turmoil. When I asked Mirwaiz Umar Farooq what in his opinion was the root cause of turbulence in Muslim societies in southern Asia, he shot back, 'Look at the double policy followed here [in Kashmir] and by other governments elsewhere ... and Muslims are very sentimental and emotional people. They cannot be bullied by any government, they react.' It seemed to me a paradoxical thing to say for someone who otherwise insisted that the problem in Kashmir was a political, not a religious one. Perhaps this too was a reflection of the change in Kashmir's Muslim population. Or perhaps I was reading too much into his words.

Giving religious overtones to the struggle in Kashmir is fraught with danger. In the mid and late 1990s, a regressive, orthodox and far less tolerant version of Islam began to grow in Kashmir, its rise coinciding with the entry of jehadi elements into Kashmir through Afghanistan and Pakistan. Some militant groups forced cinema halls and bars to shut down and began ordering women to cover themselves up in burqas. I remember being told by Kashmiri male friends a couple of years ago that I shouldn't be seen draped in a sari. 'You'll stand out,' they had snapped by way of explanation, 'and that isn't right.' The shalwar-kameez was the dress of the Kashmiri Muslim woman; only Pandit women wore saris. But Payal Abdullah (Omar Abdullah's wife) wore saris, even trousers, I insisted, to which I was told that the Abdullahs were a family of non-believers! Mercifully, the moral brigade, who even made their point by shooting a few girls who refused to wear the burqa, have quietened down, perhaps realizing that their extreme ideologies would only make them unpopular in the Valley.

Fundamentalism may not be a danger any more, but the easy tolerance that was special to Kashmir has been undermined to some extent. Signs of a subtle but definite change are unmistakable, apparent in the very lifestyle and outlook of the community. Some of the most visible changes happened abruptly, almost overnight: male friends who dressed in the trendiest of western-style suits in the late 1980s were looking like maulanas of yesteryears in 2001. When I asked them the reason, they all gave me short lectures on religion being central to everything in life. This didn't make them communal, of course—none of them were or are Hindu haters. But they put greater emphasis than ever before on projecting and guarding their Muslim identity.

It was made quite clear during any discussion on religion, for instance, that marriage or even romance with non-Muslims was out of the question. There have never been too many interfaith marriages anyway, so this new attitude seemed not only excessive but also unnecessary. There are very few well-known Hindu–Muslim couples in the Valley today, and people have something to say about each. Dr Girija Dhar and Dr Naseer Ahmad's pairing is dismissed by the locals with the rationale, 'Both of them are communists, for such people religion makes no difference.' Omar Abdullah and Payal's wedding has never been popular—in fact, for the average Kashmiri it is one more reason to dislike the Abdullahs. 'Do you know that they fight with each other constantly?' I was told. And why? 'Because she doesn't want her sons to be circumcised! Marrying outside the community is like entering hell.' The children of two prominent Kashmiri Muslim bureaucrats had recently married outside the community, and when I mentioned them to the hardliners they shrugged and said, 'These people are just *naam ka musalmaan*s, not true believers.' Unlike in the past, more and more Kashmiris feel it necessary to either condemn or dismiss interfaith alliances. Where condemnation is inconvenient, they feel the need to justify it by some absurd logic. The young, good-looking aide to the Hurriyat leaders, A. Masoodi, told me at the Hurriyat office in Delhi that he had recently married a Brahmin girl from JNU. I asked if there was any opposition. 'Not much,' I was told, 'after all, Brahmins also come from the same Aryan stock.'

One welcome result of the increased religiosity in Kashmir is a greater commitment to charity, something that Islam enjoins upon its followers. And quite a few affluent Kashmiri

Muslims do indeed seem to be supporting much needed social work: several new orphanages have been set up in Srinagar, for instance, for the orphans of the near civil war in the Valley. But despite this there is a growing class divide, more discernible among the Muslims than in any other community. I was repeatedly told that the rich aren't really involved in the day-to-day struggles. At a shop in Srinagar, a former bureaucrat's wife came in, while I was there, to place a huge order for some handicrafts to be sent to the US. As soon as she had left, the shopkeeper said to me, 'These people should be part of the movement, or at least help in saving lives, but no, they are all busy making money. In the mornings they do business and their evenings are spent playing golf.' The June 2002 issue of *Missive*, a monthly published by the Public Commission on Human Rights and edited by the lawyer-activist Parvez Imroz, carried an editorial that was a scathing attack on the rich Kashmiri Muslims:

> The economy of Kashmir has always remained an enigma for the economists. Notwithstanding the ongoing conflict, people are raising palacious [sic] houses, paying huge capitation fees to the professional colleges outside Kashmir for admission for their children... A nouveau riche class has emerged since 1989. It may be ... hawala money or black money... [And] what is more disturbing is the insensitivity and indifference of the affluent class or the upper middle class towards their fellow compatriots. Thousands of victims of violence, orphans, widows and half widows have been left to their fate. There is no community support to them ... Take the case of Gulzar Ahmad, a mine victim who lost both feet on 15 June this month in the mine blast at Kupwara and who has six children, old parents and a wife [to support]. Forgetting about his personal lifelong infirmity he has to live with, now he is worried about how to sustain the family, which

is totally dependant on him. His family need a pity [sic] sum of 1000 rupees per month for their survival, the amount spent by the kids of the affluent as pocket money in a month.

There are innumerable families who have lost not one member but 5–6 members. They are not mourning the deaths of the family members whether by security forces, renegades or militants, but are desperately struggling now to make both ends meet. There is no organized support system available ... this callous indifference is criminal, inhuman, shocking and shameful on the part of the entire community ... Take the case of the APDP which is repeatedly appealing from the last two years for adopting or at least bearing the expenses of one child of a disappeared person or for that matter donate one karnal land for raising a monument in the memory of *desaparecidos* [sic]. There has been no response from any quarter, it seems everything is superficial, as people have no commitment towards anything ... Normally in struggle or during hardship nations rise for collective efforts and the best of talent take the space, but it seems to be the reverse [in Kashmir]. One doesn't buy the argument of repression, as repression here seems to be an excuse for ... inaction.

There is another, tragic aspect of the divide between the haves and have-nots in today's Kashmir that is a direct result of militancy. It is the contrast between the renegades and the innocent citizens. The renegades have no qualms about terrorizing, even killing their co-religionists. In the name of a cause that they clearly have no commitment to, they grab land and money and settle personal scores. And the terror they unleash in the name of Kashmiri nationalism, of which religion, unfortunately, sometimes becomes a part, ensures that there are few people who will oppose them openly.

Decay

I first saw Srinagar in the black-and-white photographs my parents had taken during their honeymoon in the autumn of 1953. One of my favourite pastimes as a child was to sit with my parents' marriage album and gaze at the pines in those pictures, at the clear waters of the Chashme Shahi, the pagoda-style Sufi shrines, and the houseboats parked in a row on the Dal Lake with a couple of shikaras in the background. I fell in love with the place, and when, in 1976, I visited Srinagar for the first time, it was like returning to a childhood idyll. I stayed for a month at the MLA hostel. Looking back, it was the most carefree phase of my life. Days passed in a glow of ease and grace as I shopped at the Bund, ferried across the Jhelum, walked aimlessly up and down the Boulevard and met the who's who of the city without ever needing to make an appointment.

I still remember the time I walked into Nedou's Hotel during an afternoon walk simply to say hello to the famous owner of the place. I caught him in the middle of his lunch, but he didn't seem at all annoyed by the sudden intrusion. On the contrary, he insisted that I join him, and invited me to spend a weekend at his resort in Gulmarg. This wasn't an exception; people were generally friendly and forthcoming, though it was apparent even in those years, despite the polite and cordial interactions, that to most Kashmiris you were not from Delhi or UP or Bombay but 'from India'. The few times that the question 'Aren't you from India?' was actually spoken, it was said in a friendly sort of way; the rancour or the accusatory tone you find now wasn't there. If local shopkeepers sometimes switched to Kashmiri on purpose to pass a snide comment or two and chuckle, there would usually be someone among the non-Kashmiri shoppers who would retort with the well-known Persian verse about Kashmiris being *badzaat*, a sly race, and everybody would have a good laugh. There was no visible alienation at the time, and being 'Indian' did not work against you. The exporter-cum-artist Ghulam Moheiddin of the famous 'Suffering Moses' handicrafts outlet, I remember, had at first refused to sell me his exclusive hand-painted lampshades and had relented only when I could assure him, over half an hour or more, that I'd take good care of them and put them 'in a respectable corner of the drawing room'. When, however, the wives of a couple of local bureaucrats went the following day to buy lampshades 'exactly like those that the Indian lady picked up', they had to return empty-handed. It didn't matter to the proprietor that they were Kashmiri and obviously important people; he wouldn't part with any more of his 'beauties'.

This isn't to suggest that Kashmir in the mid-1970s was perfect. The bureaucrat-wives, both Kashmiri Pandits, for instance, were not above making communal remarks: 'If he could sell the shades to you, why not to us? ... But then you are a Muslim.' Fortunately, this grumbling and pettiness was usually the level of communal thinking in Kashmir; there was nothing more to it than religious rigidity, which actually affected a 'wayward' Muslim more than it did a person of another faith. Ramzan had started when we were in Srinagar in 1976, and suddenly, the normally friendly canteen manager did not look happy during breakfast or lunch; the look of disgust and anger on his face as the waiters served us was plainly evident. On the third or fourth day of Ramzan, he couldn't contain his anger and looking directly at me he shouted, 'I can understand these other people not fasting for Ramzan, they're not Musalmaans, but you are a Quraishi—and you still don't observe rozas! At least don't eat openly, there is something called *ehteraam* [reverence] after all!' The next day I had all my meals in my tiny bedroom. The following morning, much to my surprise, the canteen manager was at my door with a tray laden with fruit. 'Your Hindu friends told me that you are pregnant and that's why you can't fast ... I didn't know. I thought that in their company you were moving away from Islam.'

The canteen manager and I ended up becoming good friends. I discovered that he was a bit of a crank and his remark about my Hindu friends trying to influence me against Islam was easy to ignore. By the time I left Srinagar that year, he had proceeded on long leave and I was never to meet him again. When I visited the city again in 1984, this time with my two children in tow whom I took to all the places I had visited eight years earlier, he wasn't at the MLA Hostel, and the canteen itself was in a mess. Things were beginning to change. Signs of neglect and decay were clearly visible. There were murmurs about the money doled out by the Centre being eaten up by local MLAs and their kin, and there was talk of rampant corruption in the bureaucracy. One bureaucrat I knew told me that the cook attached to a particular government guest house in Raj Bagh suffered from all possible diseases that one would expect in the average pleasure-loving politician or bureaucrat. But he's just a cook, I said. 'Yes, but he tends to their needs,' the bureaucrat said, implying that in the patronage of his colourful bosses he made merry on the side too and suffered the consequences of excess. It wasn't as if Delhi, with Mrs Gandhi and then Rajiv in power, was not aware of where all its money was going. And obviously that was where Delhi wanted the money to go.

A well-known civil servant who was then working in the PMO told me that even during that period there were two different camps at the Centre, one was in favour of establishing industries in Kashmir and the other opposed this tooth and nail. The civil servant even named a minister at the Centre who would appear to be interested in any proposal for setting up factories in the Valley, would ask for the file and then sit on it. Surprisingly, none of the state-level politicians cried hoarse about the fact that the region had no industry or any other development project. They seemed content with the age-old cottage industries churning out carpets and shawls and the same old handicraft items. As long as they had their crores, they saw no reason to interfere with the callousness, or perhaps a deliberate design, of the Centre.

The big business of the state—tourism—hadn't yet shrunk considerably, but anyone could see that the decline had begun. In Pahalgam and Gulmarg the tourist huts and lodges were more than run-down. Pony-walas spoke aloud about the decrease in the number of tourists. In hushed tones they also hinted at drug trafficking in certain areas. None of this seemed to bother the politicians or bureaucrats. It was a strange kind of apathy. There was something sad and eerie about it, because on the surface things still held together but you could sense that there was rot just a few feet below.

The façade of normalcy was ripped off barely six years later. In 1990 I went to the Valley to report on the protests and violence, and the most recent major event at the time— the mass exodus of the Pandits. This was in the month of May. On my first morning in Srinagar, curfew was lifted for just an hour. I made my way towards the Boulevard, which is walking distance from Hotel Broadway where I was staying. There was the usual row of houseboats parked on the Dal, but they all looked vacant and in disrepair. It was a depressing sight, but the worst was yet to come. As I walked on, I noticed a battered shikara on the water close to the bank where the Dal Lake merges with the Jhelum river. In it were an elderly man and three children, all sitting hunched in postures of utter defeat. The man's shoulders were shaking, and as I went closer to ask if something was wrong, I realized that he was weeping. When he noticed me, he looked up, crying unashamedly and saying something loudly in Kashmiri. I couldn't understand him and asked if he could tell me in Hindustani what was wrong. He stopped speaking but continued to weep. I offered him a ten-rupee note which he brushed aside and began shouting helplessly, waving his hands around, pointing at nothing in particular. The children mumbled a few words now but I couldn't follow what they were trying to say either, and then they began pulling out weeds from the shallow waters and stuffing them into their mouths. I was aghast and stood rooted to the spot till the man wiped his face and waved me away. I walked directly towards the Bund, hoping to find my friend Ghulam Moheiddin and see if he could help. Moheiddin didn't seem surprised when I told him about the disturbing scene I had witnessed. They had no food, he explained. But they had refused the money I had offered. What did I expect, he said, they weren't beggars. Why were they eating weeds, then? 'Weeds!' Moheiddin cried out. 'Why weeds? Young lady, during the month of curfew imposed by Jagmohan even I've had to pull out weeds from the backyard and eat them. I have thousands in the bank but all of it is useless because the governor saw to it that the curfew was stretched over weeks so that even the rich like me realize the might of the state. This is tyranny unleashed on us!'

In the brief hour or two when the curfew was relaxed, people struggled desperately to stock up on essentials, and many had to rush back empty-handed. There wasn't enough of anything, and there certainly wasn't enough time to find what was scarce. The same proprietor of Suffering Moses who had refused to part with his precious handicraft wares only fourteen years back urged me this time to buy as much as possible because he had slashed his prices. He needed immediate cash. 'I have seen the days when during Maharaja Hari Singh's time there used to be such abundance of rice that stocks were thrown out—and now look at this disaster all around ...'

From the early 1990s, the deterioration in Kashmir—economic, social and psychological—has been constant and systematic. Many of the old shops may still exist, but several are mere shells, and most barely function—the proprietors are usually not around and the meagre but loyal staff try valiantly to keep some semblance of business going. Which isn't easy when guns could go off anywhere and at any time, few tourists visit the Valley, streets are deserted by sunset, and municipal services are almost non-existent. Long power cuts are a constant feature and the smell of diesel and the sound of generators working overtime follows you everywhere. On almost every trip to the Valley since the early 1990s, I have seen weavers and darners doing their job in the light of gas lamps. Of late, the young have opened commercial establishments in Srinagar to cater to new needs. Among these are cyber cafés, and here the scene has been the same for some years now—young people waiting for hours because it takes almost forever to get a 'connection' through the server located in Jammu.

Huge numbers of the young are unemployed, many more are underemployed. The principal of a school in Srinagar confessed to being frightened by the rising numbers of the jobless. 'Just last week one of my nephews told me that bekaari was making him so desperate that he might have to consider becoming a killer—the going rate for hired killers is rupees ten thousand per murder, he told me! What more can I tell you about the deterioration around?'

Bekaari, or unemployment, and the frustration of finding oneself in straitened circumstances are not the lot of everyone in Kashmir. The rich have other problems. The class divide in the Valley has become deeper since the turmoil began—there are the old rich, of course, and the very few professionals who have prospered due to their merit and financial good sense, but there are also those who have benefited from the massive corruption and other illegal activities that flourish in any region where guns talk. In the homes of most of the affluent whom I met in 2000 and again in 2002, there were at least two, sometimes three servants—young teenage boys packed off by their families in rural Kashmir so they would be out of trouble. One Kashmiri businessman told me that the boy he had employed was from Sopore and his parents had left him literally at the man's doorstep 'to keep him away from the security forces and from those other men' (by 'other men' he clearly meant militants but wouldn't use the word).

The class divide—even between the middle classes and the seriously rich—is now visible even on the streets. There are girls, for instance, who walk about with dupattas and cotton shawls duly covering their heads and chests, and then there are the famous few who can be seen in trendy jeans and tops, and, increasingly, with a gunman to protect them. Or perhaps to protect their cars. People of means in Srinagar worry constantly about their cars. In recent years car thefts have become routine. It is a minor epidemic. And nobody knows where the vehicles disappear or for what purpose. On a single afternoon in late 2002 I met three men whose cars had been stolen. One of them said to me, only half in jest, 'In your big, fashionable cities men fear losing their wives or all that it takes to keep them; here in Srinagar the poor are losing their sons, the rich their new cars ... And in both cases there's no one you can go to for lodging a complaint!'

Behind that seemingly half-serious comment there was in fact a sense of complete helplessness. At least in this respect all Kashmiris have it bad, regardless of class. In Srinagar I was told by several friends through the last decade that in case I came to any harm, was looted, or if my room was ransacked by either the security agencies or a militant group, there was nowhere I could go for immediate justice. Naturally, then, there is little or no faith in the government apparatus. Even in 1990 when I had asked a group of vocal Kashmiris why they didn't go and meet the governor, Jagmohan, and tell him about the excesses they narrated to me, they had pointed to the sky and said, 'Even birds that fly in the direction of Raj Bhavan are shot dead, so how do you think we'll get there?' If there was bitterness towards the governor and the security forces, there was ridicule for the 'sarkari' men. But the bureaucrats themselves expressed helplessness, for they too, they said, couldn't interfere with the security forces. In fact, at least four government officers told me as late as 2001 that their homes had been searched or their drivers pushed around by jawans manning check posts. 'After all, soldiers don't know whom to spare, they can't differentiate between people ... so what can we say?' was the explanation given by a bureaucrat whose official driver had been roughed up. Average Kashmiris would celebrate such incidents—more so if the bureaucrat himself were roughed up; that would be a kind of justice. I was in a village not far from Srinagar during the 2002 elections when news came in of the National Conference minister B.A. Negroo being beaten so severely by the security forces that his front teeth had been knocked out. The villagers with us cried out in absolute delight. A fellow journalist translated what they were saying: 'When we had complained to him about our boys being picked up and thrashed, he wouldn't listen—now they've broken his teeth, so he'll know!'

At a fundamental level, nothing much has changed since then, as I've noted in the last chapter. It won't be easy for any government endorsed by the Centre to build credibility in Kashmir and restore confidence among the people. The disaffection, distrust and dejection are too great. Mufti Sayeed has a tough task ahead of him, especially since the election process that brought the PDP to power has few enthusiastic supporters among Kashmiris. Democracy, they know from experience, changes meaning once you enter the Valley. On one of my tours to the interiors during the 2002 polls, two local photojournalists with whom I was sharing a jeep pointed at the Doordarshan crew filming the queue of voters at a particular polling booth in district Pulwama and sniggered. 'I can guarantee you,' one of them said, 'they'll use just this shot to show that there was a heavy turnout of voters; they'll scrap all the rest of the shots that show dismal numbers at polling booths.'

This is what Mufti Sayeed is up against. And of course, the army with its tanks is going nowhere from Kashmir, and there are many lines that the chief minister himself cannot cross.

*

As I've mentioned earlier, to get a feel of the decay in Srinagar city you only need to look around you. Each time I visit the city now, sheer disbelief keeps taking me back to the Polo Grounds where I stand and stare at the shabby, neglected building of Nedou's Hotel. There is no sign of the old life; it is as though ghosts have taken over the entire stretch. The hotel does not function any more. Security forces are now lodged in the building, but strangely even this has not ensured a facelift. The Nedou's of old crumbles, as perhaps Kashmir does, with no one bothered about the future. In both cases, it is as if no one cares to hope that things will get better tomorrow. The original owner of the hotel, Mr Nedou, is dead, and his son refused to meet me or talk on the phone. Quite by chance, I met his daughter at a bureaucrat's home, but she had more to say about her work at a spa centre in Uttar Pradesh than about the untimely death of the family hotel.

Even the lakes are decaying. The picturesque Wular Lake, once the largest lake in Asia, has shrunk from its original size of 279 sq km to only 65 sq km. The present government had sought Rs 179 crore from the Central environment ministry to launch a ten-year project to restore the lake to its old glory. What it got was approval for a short-term project of Rs 61.13 lakhs and a further Rs 50 lakhs for minor works. The more famous Dal Lake—said to be the life of the city of Srinagar—is shrinking too. Much of it is choked with weeds and garbage. An Englishmen, Charles Goschen, was concerned enough to launch the Green Kashmir Movement to save the lake—a brave initiative in a place where the environment is the least of people's concerns—but for some time now his organization has been fighting the state government in court for misappropriation of funds. This is a familiar story in Kashmir.

The houseboats, the very backbone of Srinagar's economy,

are also close to ruin. They require constant maintenance, but with tourism down to nearly zero, till early 2003 when it picked up a bit, there's no money for their upkeep. Even rich houseboat owners like G.N. Butt, who owns the Clermont houseboats, are facing tough times. Two of Butt's fleet of seven houseboats have aged prematurely. In 2001 I spent a night in one of his better-maintained houseboats. The view from that end of the Dal—the Zabarwan range at one end and Naseem Bagh at the other—was as perfect as it was over a quarter century ago, but through the night I was unable to sleep for a sinking feeling that I was experiencing the end of some tender fairy tale. I told Butt about this the next morning, and he responded by telling me about the glorious past. He spoke of the famous people who had stayed in his houseboats—Nelson A. Rockefeller, George Harrison, Yehudi Menuhin, Dilip Kumar, Pandit Ravi Shankar and several European and American envoys—and showed me the elaborate comments they had written in the visitors' notebook. He was like a child, talking of the beautiful things that once were, refusing to acknowledge the harsh truth staring him in the face. It was all as before, he wanted me to believe: the attendant, Ramzaana, still cooked up miracles in the kitchen; the shikara-man, Lassa, would still take me for a ride right up to the fishermen's village Tel Bal at the far end of the lake. Later, Butt took me to his home for dinner and opened old albums with pictures of his family dining with the rich and the famous. There was a story to each photograph and he told them all, till his daughter reminded him of his ailing mother. I saw her, too, close to death, with an end-of-an-era look on her chiselled face. Later, Butt insisted on driving me back to the houseboat, and a chowkidar who looked quite ill struggled to open the gate for us. 'That's Ahmed,' Butt said, 'only forty years old and already with a pacemaker tucked in his chest.' Then, as if he had read my mind, he explained, 'What to do! He's very ill but wouldn't accept charity and this was the only job he could do. At least you can see his illness, but we are all ill emotionally. All of us.'

I wept that night. People fall ill and die everywhere, but that night on the Dal it seemed as if every little suffering, the tiniest depletion, was a sign of a whole world dying. Butt came to see me the next morning when I was packing my bags to return to the Broadway. Why was I leaving, he asked, but I didn't have the heart to tell him. 'Please stay,' he insisted, 'pay just a third, even a fourth of the actual charges, but don't go back. These boats have been lying vacant too long, someone needs to live in them ...'

Throughout the time I was in Srinagar that year, only one of Butt's houseboats was occupied for a while. Even a year later, there were hardly any tourists in the city. When I interviewed the then director general of J&K Tourism, Mohammad Ashraf, in the autumn of 2002, he gave the dismal figures of the state's tourist trade: In 1989, there had been 722,000 tourists; in the first ten months of 2002, the figure had barely touched 30,000. 'Why is Kashmir being branded as a trouble spot?' he asked irritably. 'The attitude of the electronic media is unfortunate. After the WTC disaster the American media didn't show a single shot of a dead body, but here it is just the opposite.' Aziz Wani, the suave MD of the J&K Tourism Development Corporation, who was once a ski instructor and has seen better days as far as tourism is concerned, echoed Ashraf's opinion. And it wasn't just the media that was at fault, he said, it was also the Government of India. 'The least that GOI can do is to highlight the fact that it is safe for tourists to move around here. Nobody drags you out and shoots you, the battle is between the militants and the security forces, the tourists can be safe here.'

At least for a year after these conversations, neither the media nor GOI had done anything to encourage tourists. I visited the Clermont fleet again while I was covering the polls. From the bank, more of the houseboats looked past their prime. I could see Lassa rowing his shikara with two foreigners cuddling in it. They were the only tourists. In just a year G.N. Butt had aged considerably. His mother and granddaughter had died, and there was no sign of the chowkidar with that pacemaker, either. The cook and the attendant were still with Butt, and they too looked old. There was also a young boy from a distant village. He had been picked up by the security forces, he said. He had made it back home, bruised, with a ruptured ear drum—still alive, but who was to tell what would happen next, so he had left home and made it to Srinagar. From the manner in which he spoke to me, gathered into himself and with a tremble in his voice, it was clear that it wasn't just his body that had been bruised.

That evening Butt's younger brother, Bashir Ahmad Butt, drove in with three Italian buyers, not for the houseboats but for Kashmiri shawls. I accompanied them to one of the villages on the outskirts of the city where Bashir's relatives run a weaving centre. The village, with its apple orchards and low clouds, truly belonged in any tourist brochure promoting Kashmir as heaven on earth. In this piece of paradise I met weavers, most of them graduates, sitting hunched like ancient and unhappy grandfathers, each with a shawl in his hand. Bashir Butt's nephew took me to other weaving and embroidery centres spread out in the downtown areas of Rainawari and Nowhatta Chowk and Rajori Kadal, and there were further scenes of decay. At the first weaving centre, I met Mohammad Shafi, bent over his charkha. In recent years work had suffered, he said, and not just because there were fewer tourists and buyers. Shoot-outs, searches and arrests were also problems, but the biggest of them all was the grim power situation. They couldn't work much after dark. And with less work the daily earnings of weavers had gone down, which affected home and the hearth, and health. Another weaver, Khalil Mohammad, had been weaving designs for close to fifty years, having started as a child, but he didn't think he could go on much longer. 'My chest has given up,' he wheezed. 'I can't breath. I have no energy left in these limbs. Earlier I regularly worked till late night but not now ... and anyway there's no electricity.' Elsewhere, two brothers were doing intricate embroidery for an American designer, Judy Ross, but their faces were devoid of any pride or any emotion at all. They spoke only after much pleading. Life was hard, they told me, and what was there to say. 'We have been beaten so many times by the security forces that there's no desire to speak or shriek now ... We keep on doing this chain stitch the entire day, in the evenings we have to stop as there's no power and then we lie down somewhere here and wait for the next morning. Earlier, this room used to be full of workers and we worked till ten at night ... but then those searches began and everything changed. *Humko kuchh samajh nahin aata hai ke yeh log kya chahte hain. Zulm kar rahen hain.* [We don't understand what these people want. They spread terror.]'

As Bashir Butt's nephew and I walked in silence to the other weaving and embroidery units, the embroidery patterns differed but the stories we heard were the same. One artisan who travelled daily from Anantnag said that he was fed up with the unending searches. 'Most men of my age group working here—thirty, thirty-five years old—most have heart problems. Much of my daily earnings of fifty rupees is spent on medicines ... *Par shukar hai zinda hun* [But at least I'm alive].' At the weaving centre close to the Idgah, Mohammad Yaseen Hakar told me about how the turmoil and the completely unpredictable searches conducted by the army had affected him, and then he asked me to guess his age. Sixty, sixty-five, I guessed. No, he said quietly, he was only forty-eight. The shock must have shown on my face, because he explained: 'How would your brother or father feel if he was thrashed by cops in full view of his family—his wife and children. The first few times it happened I would cry, but now I'm too tired even for that. I have no energy for anything ... and see my hands? Twisted with arthritis.' He, too, spent most of what he earned on medicines, though this didn't guarantee relief either. I had been told that the spurious drug trade was rampant in Kashmir. A *Times of India* report of 30 January 2003 later confirmed this:

> The health sector in Kashmir is faced with the problem of unregulated flow of sub-standard and spurious drugs to 1,800 unregistered medical stores ... of the 2,100 medical shops in the valley only 300 are registered with the office of the drug controller. A druggist, Habibullah Lone of Haftchinar, blames the drug controller for the delay in grant of licences to chemists. Lone's application for a license is pending with the office of the drug controller since 1976 ...

The government didn't seem concerned enough about the weavers' problems, so in 1999 thirty of them got together and set up an association of weavers and embroiderers to manage their own needs, but it hasn't got a registration yet. The file is probably lying forgotten on some babu's desk.

*

Kashmir is a diminished society. Most of the Pandits have left, and that is an absence anyone who has seen Kashmir before 1990 will notice most easily. But there are other absences. Public space has shrunk; the ease of life is long gone, and the open, outgoing Kashmiri is nowhere to be seen. After the initial passionate defiance of 1989, after the men in uniform moved in, the battered populace began retreating—more every passing year. This was not a sign of submission, but of gloom, coupled with a bitterness of the worst kind.

In troubled times, people find solace in faith. I have seen women—'half widows' and mothers—wailing in the ziarats, the shrines of Sufi saints, praying for the safe return of their husbands or sons who disappeared without a trace, and old men sitting around with a vacant look in their eyes. More recently, I've seen women at the ziarats begging for money—something unheard of in the past. Cynics in the administrative system told me that like the 'imported' maulvis even these beggar women had come to the Valley from UP and Bihar! I spoke to six such women, and they were all Kashmiris, each with her own horror story—someone's home had been burnt down, another's sons had gone missing and she had no support system, and there was a half widow hoping to collect enough money to travel to Jodhpur. 'The pir sahib at this ziarat has said that he's in the Jodhpur jail ... I've already spent what I had travelling to Delhi, Jammu and Agra, looking for him.'

But only the truly desperate seem to frequent the ziarats now. In a decade, the old faith, too, seems to have changed. A unique culture, born of Sufi Islam, is clearly on the decline. The violence in the Valley, the anger and despair of the Kashmiris, especially the younger generation, has affected even the traditional systems of belief. There is a hardening of attitudes, a preoccupation—perhaps inevitable—with the politics of the present and the immediate past; few have the time or mental space for other aspects of their history and culture. Which, of course, makes the job of jehadi outfits, based outside the Valley, that much easier.

The average Kashmiris, caught up as they are in the harsh realities of everyday life, don't seem to know the relevance of their own patron saints. It is 'outsiders' who are making efforts to understand and promote the vision and the work of Kashmir's saints and poets. Jalabala Vaidya and Gopal Sharma have made a film on Sheikh Nooruddin Wali (Nand Rishi), highlighting the relevance of his teachings in the present time of turmoil. Muzaffar Ali has devoted years of his life to an unfinished film on the life of the legendary Kashmiri poet Habba Khatun. The classical dancer Sonal Mansingh has tried to interpret through dance the mysticism of the saint-poet Lal Ded. The Kashmiri establishment, meanwhile, makes cosmetic gestures like naming one of its maternity set-ups after Lal Ded.

Today, Sufi saints of the past mean less to Kashmiris than the present-day pirs, mostly ordinary Muslim men posing as religious figures. The gentle, tolerant spirit of Sufism is losing out to rigid, orthodox versions of Islam. Even in the mid-1990s, when I travelled to different ziarats—from Shah-i-Hamadan and Dastgeer Sahib to Maqdoom Sahib and Charar-i-Sharief—I was urged to make a wish and tie the *mannat* thread. But in recent years this has rarely happened. I remember sitting in the compound of the dargah of Shah-i-Hamadan in 2002 one afternoon—there were hardly any worshippers there. It was tranquil; even the security guards were at a distance, keeping an eye on the few people feeding the pigeons. I sat quietly on the steps leading to the Jhelum. Perhaps Shah-i-Hamadan, the Iranian Syed, had crossed this river during his flight to the Valley to escape the wrath of

Timur. The Valley had given him refuge, peace and reverence; he had never gone back to the country of his origin. Many others like him had come here from Iraq and the Central Asian republics, fleeing the tyranny of their fanatical rulers who preferred a different version of Islam. And now people were fleeing *from* the Valley; it wasn't a place of refuge for anyone any more. Later that afternoon I was joined at the ziarat by a couple of college students. They were both Kashmiri Muslims who stayed not too far away, in the downtown area, but they knew nothing about this Sufi who had played a significant role in shaping the lives of thousands, and whose verse is still sung but rarely understood. (Few young Kashmiris sing the verses of the saints today. I met a young man who prefers reciting one of his own: one in praise of electricity! As a struggling publisher in Srinagar explained, for people like him, whose work depended on electricity, and the power situation being dismal, electricity was as dear as one's mother.)

Meanwhile, the culture brigade and the event managers in places like Delhi are cashing in on the Sufi music of Kashmir. None of them have the courage to carry their programmes, or even some of the harvest they reap from them, to the people of Jammu and Kashmir.

*

On 13 October 2002, I met three new interns at the government hospital for mental health in Srinagar. They were not very comfortable answering my questions till I asked them about how the people they treated were coping with the situation. People were coping, they said, as they themselves did. 'Everybody is enveloped in it—perhaps that's the only consolation. We're doctors, but circumstances have affected us too... everybody suffers from post-traumatic stress.'

The following morning at the hospital I saw the long queue at the OPD. Most of the patients were subdued but the image of one patient haunts even now. She was a middle-aged lady who kept begging everyone for a rupee. When I asked what her problem was, she looked heavenwards and chanted, '*Kul-e-alam ka gham* [The pain of the world].' She kept up the chant, and forgot about the rupee she wanted.

The most widespread and disturbing sign of the decay in Kashmir today is the vast number of psychologically disturbed people. The brochure of one of the 'foreign bodies' operating in the Valley—Médecins Sans Frontières—says, 'The violence in one way or the other has touched each family living in Kashmir and this is having a profound effect on the overall well-being of people here.' According to psychiatrists working in the Valley, 90 per cent of the population is emotionally disturbed. The number of patients at the OPD of the lone government hospital for psychiatric diseases in the Valley increased from six a day in 1990 to an average of 250–350 patients a day in 2000. According to the hospital records, the total number of patients rose from 1760 in 1990 to 18,000 in 1994 and to over 38,000 in 2001. This is only the number of those who could make it to this hospital. For a population of nearly five million there is just this one hospital for the psychologically damaged. And it has no lab, no x-ray facilities, no separate rooms for patients, and no woman psychiatrist. The outer walls of the building are charred—it was partially burnt down in 1994. Inside, patients are stuffed like sardines in general wards, and makeshift rooms have been converted into OPDs. None of this should surprise one, given that the psychiatrist-patient ratio in the Valley is 1:200,000, as reported in the January–March 2001 issue of *JK Practioner*.

When I asked one of the psychiatrists, outside whose makeshift room there was the longest queue, what segment of the population seemed most affected, he replied, 'Ask who isn't affected. Thirteen years of turbulence has affected everyone—after all, there is only so much human beings can cope with. The most visibly affected are children and the women. There is an alarming increase in the number of suicide attempts, as reflected in the psychiatric outpatient population, especially amongst adolescent girls and young women from the rural areas. The majority of them have no previous history of psychiatric disorders.' A large percentage of those who queue up suffer from post-traumatic stress disorder (PTSD). A study conducted by psychiatrists of the hospital concluded:

PTSD can be a chronic and disabling condition but has not been studied much against a backdrop of 12 years of armed militant uprising in the Kashmir Valley ... We present here the first such report of a treatment-seeking sample...

The patients in the sample were mostly illiterate, from a lower socio-economic status and more than half were married. The illness tended to be severe with a mean duration of 40 months. 20% had been tortured, 36% had had close relatives killed violently in front of them, and 30% per cent had been injured in shoot-outs and grenade explosions and the like ... Levels of morbid depression and anxiety were high... there is a great need to recognize PTDS early and develop effective therapeutic modalities suitable to our culture for what may be a disorder of epidemic proportions in the valley.

Doctors in Srinagar have always been very vocal about the situation in the Valley. Even as early as 1990, a large group of doctors—there were Muslims, Christians and Hindus in the group—had tracked me down at Hotel Broadway and spoken candidly about the tragic consequences of the shootings and beatings, cases that they attended to regularly. In 2002 again, they were outspoken, despite what one of them told me—that the orthopaedic specialist Dr Farooq Ashai, he believed, had been killed because he was vocal about the 'battered state' of the patients being brought to his hospital. This time the doctors had as much to say about psychological damage as they did about the victims of shoot-outs.

An alarmingly large number of children, I was told, suffered from psychological problems. During the autumn of 2002, the day I shifted from the Tourist Reception Centre to a lovely guest house by the Jhelum, there was a spurt of intense but enthusiastic activity at the guest house. This is rare in Srinagar, so I asked the young Assamese caretaker what the fuss was all about. 'The Rajiv Gandhi Foundation people are coming by today's afternoon flight,' he said. I decided to wait for their arrival in the front lawns. They turned out to be a rather cheerful group of counsellors and psychologists from New Delhi. Later, I learnt that they had been coming to the Valley regularly, training schoolteachers in the Valley to reach out and help their young students cope with stress. One of them, Bindu Prasad, a clinical psychologist, had been training fifty-five teachers in the Badgam district, a majority of them Muslims and a few Sikhs. 'What we are trying to do is to build hope,' she said. 'But if the environment doesn't change, we can only try and lower the levels of suffering and stress.' Her colleague Kishwar Ahmad Shirali who makes frequent trips to Srinagar to counsel orphaned children, said that since 1998 she had noticed that people were less traumatized, but this could change at any time, because the basic issues hadn't gone away. It was clear that people in the Valley still wanted independence, she said, and it was also clear that they weren't going to get it.

So the confrontations and searches and militant strikes and human rights abuse continue. A report by the journalist-photographer team of Sreedharan and Jewella Miranda details how a painting competition provided evidence of how this has left scars on the minds of the young:

There were 495 children at the competition. All normal school-going youngsters. Of normal, conscientious parents. Sprawled out all over the grassy ground that sunny morning, partaking in Srinagar's first painting competition in nearly ten years, they drew with passion. First the brisk, light pencil sketches. Then the bolder crayon strokes. On 495 sheets of paper, their dream Kashmir—'My Valley'— was coming alive. But not many were of that paradise on earth, the Kashmir of unsurpassed beauty. Not many were of snow-clad mountains and lush green valleys. The majority, instead, were of the Kashmir of violence, the Kashmir of turbulence. Of guns, grenades and gore. And mujahid [militant], kabr [grave], and shaheed [martyr] ... The paintings opened a window to the scarred psyche of the children of Kashmir, the children of conflict. Many— probably a majority—of the children in Kashmir [not just the 10,000-odd orphans of militancy but the average school-going, normal kids] have deep permanent bruises of the mind ... that have far-reaching consequences, that are now finding reflection in psychic disorders, drug abuse and personality changes. Medical statistics confirm this.

Dr Altaf Hussain, a leading paediatrician of Srinagar, confirmed what the report said. The children had been cheated of their childhood, he said. 'They haven't been able to play, go on picnics or even just walk in the open without fear. All this repression is bound to manifest itself sooner or later ... mental health is not easily quantifiable, but I would say that over 60 per cent of the children have been bruised badly.'

Yet few people or organizations have actually taken the trouble to reach out and do something not only for the children but also the women and men who are in urgent need of help and counselling. There are some human rights activists who frequent the Valley, but very few others are working to actually improve living conditions. Even back in 1995 I was so appalled by the lack of sensitivity that I'd written about it in the *Times of India* of 18 May 1995:

> I noticed a total absence of counselling centres, therapists and voluntary agencies ... such an acute absence of voluntary agencies in a terrorism-ravaged state has sent depression-related cases soaring. Doctors at the government hospital for psychiatric diseases at Saida Kadal confirmed during my last visit that at least 400 depression-related cases and a rising number of epilepsy cases came in every day. Even the Army spokesperson at Srinagar admitted that they had no counselling units for the jawans ...

After first witnessing the human disasters in Srinagar some years ago, I had naively asked several worthies heading big-time NGOs in Delhi about what kept them from working in the Valley. None had any clear answers. Only Pramila Dandavate of the Mahila Dakshata Samiti gave me a reason I could understand: 'We need financial assistance, then the locals have to take up the responsibility, for I believe that the situation there is such that even officers are not willing to get posted, so how can our volunteers go?' There were also some NGO types who said that the people of the Valley had revolted, so where was the need to reach out to them? I would not have believed that this degree of callousness is possible had I not heard more than one person say this to me. Today, fortunately, there are several local trusts manning orphanages and educational institutions in the Valley, but there are no NGOs working with the emotionally disturbed. The few exceptions are the volunteers (mostly locals) working for Rajmohan Gandhi's Centre for Dialogue and the counsellors of the Rajiv Gandhi Foundation who have been running two projects at the grass-roots level. Of late, ActionAid India, the Guild of Service and OXFAM have also begun projects in the Valley. But these hardly add up to an accessible platform where a disturbed teenager or a distraught woman or even a harassed man can go and seek help.

The international presence in the Valley is marginal. The UN Office on Gupkar Road has zero powers and its presence is mere tokenism. Besides this, there are just two 'foreign bodies' (the Centre's favoured term for such organizations) functioning in Kashmir, but with very limited roles: International Council of the Red Cross and Doctors Without Frontiers (DWF)/Médecins Sans Frontières. The jurisdiction of the former is limited to visiting jails and interacting with those detained, and there has been criticism by several Kashmiri activists who point out that the ICRC has compromised its credibility by agreeing to a token presence in the Valley. They say this insignificant presence has actually helped the Indian government's cause, in the sense that the latter can now claim that it has allowed independent international observers to monitor the situation in the Valley on a regular basis. When I met Georgios Georgantas in 2002, he didn't deny the limited jurisdiction. Under the memorandum of understanding signed between the Government of India and ICRC in June 1995, the latter is allowed access only to the detention centres and prisons in Jammu and Kashmir. The committee's mandate: to assess the prevailing conditions in the detention centres and look at the treatment meted out to the prisoners. But in fact the

ICRC team can do little to improve conditions and bring about relief for the prisoners because they cannot interfere with the manner in which the prisoners are dealt with and treated.

My meeting with the young counsellors attached to DWF was disappointing. Their role, too, is limited, and as one of them admitted, they follow the pattern laid out by the Voluntary Health Association of India, funded by the health ministry. When I met them in October 2002, they were running two health-care centres: one in Ganderbal and another in the Pulwama district and also assisting in the OPD of the Government Hospital for Psychiatric Diseases in Srinagar. They were tight-lipped about their limited jurisdiction and also about the 'self-imposed curfew' and the ground realities in the Valley vis-à-vis the mental and physical health of the people there. As their Canadian counsellor Lynne Chobotar told me, in an extremely cautious manner, 'My assessment is that women are really getting affected because they are living in fear—of violence taking place and of they themselves or, more likely, their sons and husbands being affected by it ... Recently, in the Pulwama district hospital a woman tried to commit suicide by consuming insecticide.' She also said that the women 'are still sometimes physically searched by security men and they hate this the most'. She thought it incredible that for a population of five million people there were only six government psychiatrists and just one such hospital. 'Each one of the doctors is greatly committed,' she said, 'in spite of the fact that he is overworked.'

What Lynne was cautious not to say was that this could never be enough, that the government didn't care, and that most people outside the Valley could not even begin to imagine the stress levels arising out of the constant threat of violence. Just how much violence and callousness has seeped into the Kashmiri fabric, to what extent individuals and society as a whole have degenerated, became evident to me one morning in the mid-1990s. It is now over six years since this happened, but I remember it as if it happened yesterday. I was in Aligarh to interview Aligarh Muslim University's new vice chancellor, Mehmood-ur-Rahman, a senior bureaucrat from the J&K cadre. At the appointed time, close to noon, I walked into his office, sat down opposite him and took out my diary and pen. Meanwhile, he, to my horror, took out a revolver—loaded, I'm certain, going by the smug, almost amused expression on his face. Quite unnecessarily and very deliberately, he placed it on the table, right in front of me. 'I'm from the J&K cadre,' he said coolly, 'I'm used to dealing with terrorists, so I always carry a revolver. For my own protection.' It did not surprise me when I heard, soon after, that several students of the university complained that he treated them as though they were terrorists too.

The Lost Romance

During my 2002 trip to Srinagar at the time of the polls, I met Johnson Thomas, a young priest from Kerala attached to the Diocese Society of Jammu and Kashmir and also vice principal of Srinagar's Burn Hall School. Talking about Kashmiri society, he said to me, 'Though I have been in the state for the last three years I'm still intrigued by the popular saying that Kashmiri men are as unpredictable as the Kashmiri weather. In fact, I'm reading books and doing a field study on this unpredictability aspect.'

Perhaps he was intrigued because he took the old remark too literally. I have been travelling to the Valley since 1976, and have never felt let down by either its weather or its men. If you have interacted with them long enough, you realize that Kashmiris are highly emotional people, with an air of romanticism about them. Given the natural beauty and the difficult history of the region, this shouldn't be surprising. To me, it has been further evidence of the warmth and the charm of the Valley.

I remember the time I interviewed the ailing JKLF chief Yasin Malik at the Hurriyat headquarters—now sealed—in New Delhi's Malviya Nagar. He seemed not so much the hard-core militant that the Government of India portrayed him as, but rather a diehard romantic fading rather prematurely into oblivion. He recited verses from the tragic actress Meena Kumari's famous poem 'Tanhai'—Loneliness— and because he had recently suffered a partial paralysis, the words sounded impossibly sad. He spoke less of politics and more of his student days, and that turning point at the age of seventeen when he made a poster with the word 'Azadi', or independence, painted on it and was beaten and imprisoned for the offence. That meeting with him culminated over lunch, with the present vice chancellor of the Jammu University, Amitabh Mattoo, also joining us, and between them the two Kashmiri men, with their easy manner and charming ways, transformed the simple vegetarian lunch into a special affair. Some months later I met Shabir Shah, one of the first in Kashmir to take on the establishment (his father Ghulam Mohammed Shah's death in 1989 was the first custodial death in the Valley). He was surprisingly suave, at times a bit excessively so. Sitting in the office of the Jammu Kashmir Democratic Freedom Party in Raj Bagh, he spoke about oppression and the resistance, dressed in a well-cut corduroy jacket, smelling strongly of some expensive deodorant. It all appeared a bit incongruous. (I remember one of his former aides joking about his manner: 'Perhaps some foreign agency sent him to one of the finishing schools in Europe—in eastern Europe, more likely!') I noticed this casual refinement not just in the Hurriyat men but also in two hard-core commanders of the Hizbul Mujahideen, M.A. Untoo (who now runs an NGO, Human Rights Front) and Imran Rahi, both of whom I ran into quite by chance. I was well aware of their reputation, but I never felt threatened.

Travelling in the Valley, I have walked unescorted on the roads of Srinagar, in the narrow lanes and by-lanes of the city, and never felt unsafe. The only time I did was in 2002; I was out late (7 p.m., in fact, but late by Srinagar standards) and near Raj Bagh a teenager walked up and tried to snatch my handbag. A Sikh gentleman appeared within seconds and that put an end to the boy's feeble attempts to rob me. The gallant Sikh escorted me to the hotel and explained that this sort of thing happened sometimes these days because of the rising numbers of drug addicts in Srinagar.

Moving around in Srinagar and the surrounding villages I encountered time and again the peculiar, almost old-fashioned chivalry of Kashmiri men. One of them would invariably offer me a seat in a crowded bus, there would be no pushing or groping. And when I travelled with local journalists, they would insist on paying the bill whenever we stopped for tea or snacks. I protested in the beginning, and suggested that we go Dutch, to which they laughed and said, 'We are Kashmiri men and not like your Dilli ones—it is our duty to look after women.' Sometimes, the attention bordered on flirtation, but it was harmless, made mild by an old-world charm. The proprietor of the bakery Lala Shaikh, I remember, seemed absurdly concerned about my sore throat, and gave me ginger cookies containing 'ingredients good enough to eliminate any virus in the throat'. At the STD booth just off Maulana Azad Road, the wrinkled man at the counter would waive payment for short calls with a smile and a poetic line: 'Yeh silsila chalta rahe, aap aate raho [May this relationship continue, so you'll keep coming back].' It was all very quaint, nothing more than charming gestures—it was obvious they would forget all about me till I returned the next time. And they all seemed to know, instinctively, where the line was that they couldn't cross, so it never occurred to me to take offence.

Perhaps I had it easy because I was an outsider. No one, for instance, was inquisitive about the private life of a single woman travelling alone through the Valley. Unlike in Delhi.

Whatever the reason, I have felt freer and more alive in Kashmir—more in the past than in recent years—as have numerous other women I know. This, after all, was where legendary women like Lal Ded and Habba Khatun had led phenomenal lives—leaving husbands and homes to wander about the countryside, singing songs of devotion and divine love. Kashmir, in fact, has been home to more poets and seers than any other place in this part of the world, which seems natural when you are in the Valley, because on a day when you can forget the blood and tears that are the fate of Kashmir today, you discover romance in every little aspect of life there. Going down the highway towards Pampore and onwards to Romo village in Pulwama district in a car, I asked S.K. Dhar who was at the wheel whether I would be able to see saffron flowers. He shook his head and said something that multiplied the special romance of Kashmir several times: 'No, we won't see them. For some inexplicable reason the flowers first bloom only on Puran Mashi, the night of the full moon.'

Will this romance last, this romance in the very air of the place, if not in the lives of its people? I have asked my Kashmiri friends this question on several occasions in the last couple of years. All of them, without exception, have shaken their heads dismally. 'There is too much that has been brutalized,' one of them said. Another explained, 'There is so much frustration, and it is on the rise ... Even the men—true, you still won't hear of our men dragging women out and molesting them, but times are changing.' It was the same story—'no one knows who is who any more'. The Kashmiri may not have been corrupted and debased yet, but the 'Kashmiri cause' has been exploited for almost a decade now by men who have no connection with the Valley. Residents of the Valley will not believe one of their own capable of any serious mischief, leave alone the kind of horrors we read about so often—bomb blasts, abductions, rape and extortion. But the perception elsewhere is changing. And then, how long does sanity and gentleness survive in a place in the grip of fear and random violence for years?

Human relationships and sexuality come under strain in times of turmoil and in societies where freedom of movement and expression is restricted. Given this, it is surprising that Srinagar remains one of the few cities in the world without a red-light district, at least not an identifiable one. There is constant talk now of certain houseboats and houses where sex is offered for money or other favours. Are the men who frequent these places civilians, security personnel, tourists or militants? The locals wouldn't elaborate. A college lecturer who I had been told gossiped readily to her colleagues about the sexual 'bandobast' for the city's who's who, clammed up when I asked her about it. She blushed furiously and mumbled, 'I don't know much ... It's just that these activities are taking place in particular areas, men who want to commit that kind of sin know where to go.' A well-known National Conference MLA seemed less reticent on the subject. Didn't I know, he asked, and then spoke with great concern about reports he had heard that a small number of schoolgirls had got involved in a prostitution racket. He even told me of a girl being caught red-handed with a fat bundle of currency notes, but refused to say anything about the men who were using her services, hinting that he could get killed if he did. Sometimes, though, things came out into the open almost by accident: shortly before the 2002 elections, there was much hue and cry over a newspaper report about two police officials who were caught in the act in a city hotel.

In Srinagar's medical college, I interviewed medical professionals manning the National AIDS Control office in the city. The two senior doctors I met gave me conflicting opinions. Dr M. Masoodi, the coordinator for NACO (the AIDS control project, incidentally, began in J&K only in 2002) at first looked thoroughly ill at ease at my questions, and then conceded, 'It is supposed to happen in some houseboats, but this is not a confirmed fact.' His junior, Dr Khurshid Qureshi, was categorical that all such talk was rubbish. I asked him then about studies that suggest that family life and conventional morality anywhere come under obvious strain in times of turmoil. 'The Kashmiri family is intact,' he retorted. 'Actually, because of the depressing circumstances there's a decrease in sexual activity—tell me, who can think of sex if there's firing going on all the time? This theory must be true for developed countries but not for us ... I live in Ganderbal, which is a forty-five-minute drive from Srinagar and often on my way home I'm stopped by the security forces, many a time I've been ordered to put my hands up to be frisked, I have to prove my identity, though I'm a doctor attached to this government medical college. Now tell me, if someone like me reaches home after all this humiliation, do you think he's in any kind of mood for sex even with his spouse?' About 'straying' outside the home, they were quite clear—it was unimaginable in Kashmiri society. This was clearly just conviction, not the result of any survey or study they had done. Their vehemence startled me— one of them even said something about the fires of hell—and I was alarmed to think that these men were running the AIDS programme in the state.

Another young doctor, who also has the distinction of opening the first snooker parlour in Srinagar, Dr Zubair Ashai, was more reasonable. 'I have no steady woman friend, but those who do have girlfriends are finding it frustrating. The only place they can meet even to talk is a friend's home because the security chaps are always prying around. They clearly can't meet in their own homes because we are still a rather conservative society.' He accepted that extramarital affairs were entirely possible—they happened in the past and they were happening now. 'Today they're definitely on the rise,' he said. 'Perhaps that's the only way people can relax; after all, this generation of Kashmiris never had a chance to grow normally.'

A Sikh businessman living without his wife in Srinagar made an observation about the old romance having been leached out of young lives in the city. 'Those sly romances are over, the charm is gone. Young people seem desperate now, even the girls. You can see it on their faces.' There was a joke doing the rounds that the then chief minister, Farooq Abdullah, was concerned about the rising levels of frustration among the youth and had ordered his special STF men not to disturb youngsters in the Botanical Gardens, but would land up there himself!

Jokes aside, it is true that as a woman you rarely feel comfortable being seen with a man, even a casual acquaintance you want to just talk to, or, as in my case, someone you want to interview. This, at least, is not new. Srinagar is a small place, a closed society, and even a simple act of having a cup of coffee with a man whom you are not related to will be noticed and talked about. The day after I had met a senior doctor, for instance, I was amused when Kashmiri friends asked in a roundabout manner if I was unwell and if the prescription the good doctor had written for me in a coffee shop had helped (it was, in fact, some Urdu verse that the doctor had written out on the napkin). Then there was the evening when a well-known politician of the city who had to take me along to meet people in his constituency waited for sunset before he drove out with me.

Shameem Abdullah, a Kashmiri settled in New Delhi, explained that this was not unusual. 'Just the age-old tradition of women not going out openly with strangers,' she said. 'Call it small-town norms.' But I discovered that in Kashmir today there was more to this than just small-town discretion. A senior civil servant told me bluntly, 'An adult male and female together don't go unnoticed by the cops. They get suspicious if you aren't related—especially if a local man is seen with a woman who is an outsider. Teenagers can get away with it, perhaps, but not people of our age group.' So there's secrecy about things where there needn't be any.

There is also a new, unnecessary conservatism, the kind that you see in societies under siege where religious orthodoxy becomes a part of the attitude of dissent. I found it disappointing to meet students of Srinagar University who reacted rather fiercely to any queries related to romance or sex. Several of them didn't bother to hide their disgust: how dare I even think of these things when azadi was the only true concern. I saw a few young couples sitting under the gigantic chinars or huddled under the canopies of the restaurants in the university campus, but they denied this had anything to do with something as frivolous and vulgar as romance. A final-year commerce student, Irfan Ahmad, startled me when he said with a strange sense of bravado, 'No girlfriend for me, I'm a Muslim!'

Perhaps I really was being unrealistic, expecting to hear anything about love and companionship in these troubled times. The old honeymooners' Kashmir doesn't exist any more. The young are fiercer idealists than those mellowed by age and experience. Instead of showing me their love nests, a group of ten final-year students of the university took me to a room in one corner of the city from where they run a small office to help those in distress. I watched their earnest faces and wondered about the harsh realities of everyday life they must have witnessed and experienced to have reached such maturity so early. Fauzia writes regularly on human rights violations in one of the local newspapers. The others talk of what they see every day—the plight of innocents imprisoned in Srinagar's central jail, families that can't be together because young boys have to be packed off to safer addresses, financial lows, homes transformed into mini battlefields as husbands and wives come undone due to the constant tension and turn on each other. Some of them have seen men being shot at but haven't been able to go up and help them as they lay dying; others have had to frequently suffer lewd comments from STF men and swallow their rage. It saddened me to see them, looking older than they were, all dressed in simple cotton attires, all unsmiling.

The teachers are unable to draw these students out and give them hope. As the head of the foreign languages department who is also the president of the Kashmir University Teacher Association, Professor Bashir Ahmad, said to me, 'There's the politics of fear prevailing in this place. As a teachers' body there's little we can do. Personally, I seem to have aged prematurely—I am forty-six but look much older … I've been losing weight, can't concentrate on my work, my family life is a mess. My wife was injured in a blast in Lal Chowk recently.' His colleague, Dr Noor Mohammad Bilal, added, 'If human dignity is choked and abused, nothing remains. There's no space for finer emotions. It's been a tension-ridden life for us all. My own brother was picked up for questioning and taken to an interrogation centre where he was subjected to electric shocks in his private parts. A colleague and a close friend, Javed Ahmad, was shot dead point-blank at Dastgeer Sahib for no apparent reason and though we approached the governor who is also the chancellor of the university, nothing happened. My neighbour Rafiq Ahmad Bakal was killed at Kokar bazar by an officer ... I can go on and on. So don't talk to us about love and our personal lives!'

The present situation in the Valley has also resulted in several men remaining single for much longer than ever before, and it would be a mistake to assume that this has no effect on the traditional Kashmiri society. During my most recent travels I met men in their early forties who were single and not inclined to marry either. Some said that even if they did marry, they wouldn't like to have children in the present scenario.

In 2001, even the well-to-do Amla brothers had told me exactly the same thing. Many of the separatist leaders themselves married very late or, like Yasin Malik, have remained unmarried. Shabir Shah, one of those who have spent more years inside jail than out of it, told me in 2002, 'I am forty-six years old, and I've been in jails for over twenty-three years. Obviously, this factor alone has affected my personal life—couldn't complete my studies, got married only three years back.' The lawyer activist Parvez Imroz, who set up the APDP, also married late. Dr Rauf, at thirty, does not even think of marrying and has taken up the responsibility of running Srinagar's biggest orphanage, Yateem Trust. Forty-two-year-old Irfan Hassan, a former SI of the J&K Police who resigned in 1987, says it is inconceivable that he would marry, given the abnormal living conditions in the Valley ... The list goes on.

Quite a number of those who were once married, and are not any more for various reasons, would also risk loneliness than a remarriage. Ameen Laharwal, a former senior bureaucrat who after retirement took over as principal of a public school, talked constantly about loneliness and yet he brushed aside even the notion of remarriage. 'It's okay for Europeans to think in these terms but not for us—here we are old at forty, and these days even earlier ... we have to overcome loneliness by turning religious!'

The saddest lives, of course, are those of the 'half widows', whose numbers run into the thousands. They can't remarry because of the suspense involved. Their husbands disappeared—picked up by the security forces or militants or done away with by enemies who take advantage of the uncertain times—but their bodies were never found. These women have no choice but to wait, many of them eking out a miserable existence. In a donga parked at one end of the Jhelum, I witnessed the numbing tragedy of the half widows: beautiful, sad-eyed Shareefa and her three children, looking out of the low window of the donga with tired hope in their eyes. The man of the house, an auto driver, Abdul Hamid Badyari, was picked up for interrogation in January 2000 and there has been no news of him since. 'He might be alive,' Shareefa whispers, 'I'll wait for him.' Meanwhile, she works as a part-time domestic help.

There are close to six thousand women waiting for their husbands or sons to return.

*

And yet there is a general perception that the stress and insecurity have also brought families together. Streets empty out at dusk, as men and women scurry back home and stay confined inside their homes through the long evenings and through the night, till it is light again. They take out the prayer mat, or gather in front of the television. These are abnormal routines, not the happy gatherings of close-knit families. At Srinagar's hospital for psychiatric diseases I had been told that most families had members suffering from post-traumatic stress; long hours with each other were unable to heal them. Interpersonal relationships, even 'biological functions', were affected. One patient spoke of the constant, oppressive atmosphere of gloom at home; a doctor talked reluctantly about decreased libido, and another confided that because of the tension his wife had developed a skin ailment that had destroyed her spirit and affected their relationship.

Dr Mushtaq Margoob, the head psychiatrist summed it up for me: 'Family life has been adversely affected. What else do you expect when ninety per cent of the population is emotionally disturbed? Sooner or later human beings reach a stage where they cannot cope with abnormal conditions—and here this situation has been stretched for over thirteen years. There's been a six-fold increase in suicide attempts. When the effect of medicines fades, they turn to religion and while that helps many of my patients, it doesn't help everyone.'

Religion has indeed become more visible in the recent past. It is undeniable that a certain rigidity has crept in; there is something less traditionally Kashmiri, less attractive about religious attitudes now. It is not just about men wearing skull-caps, women pulling their dupattas tight over their heads and round their torsos, and thousands rushing to the mosque, so much so that on Fridays the namaazis spill out onto the roads. It is more about a worrying number of people doubting your sincerity unless you wear your Islamic identity on your sleeve; it is about some militant outfits threatening girls with death and disfigurement unless they cover themselves up in burqas; it is about fiery young students defending the Taliban and everything about Saddam Hussain for no reason other than their shared faith and what they see as the valour of these men.

But it would be unfair to ignore the positive power of this increased faith. It is undeniable that there is also a humbling strength, to endure the worst and to do good, which comes to a majority of ordinary people through their faith. Dr Mushtaq Margoob has had several offers to work abroad or in other cities of the country but he will not leave the Valley. 'I am answerable to Him,' he said simply. 'I see 300 to 400 patients every day in my OPD ... it is my duty as a human being ... that is what God wants me to do.' The young dentist Dr Rauf Mohi-u-deen who runs Yateem Trust for orphaned boys also sees it as a divine mission. He seeks no government grants and sustains the project through donations from his doctor colleagues. I asked him if he had been inspired by Mother Teresa, and he shook his head. 'No, I'm inspired only by Islam. I have never been closer to my faith than I am now. It is Islam that makes me do all this for these forty-seven boys who have lost their fathers to the ongoing turbulence.' I had similar reactions from the most unexpected people.

The BBC's Srinagar correspondent, Altaf Hussain, whose home in the journalist colony of Pratap Park had been recently raided twice by the army, was keen that I understand how much his faith mattered to him, every day of his life. 'I'm able to take these trials and strains in my stride because of the strength my faith offers me. It's the same for my family, my wife and three children.' Meeting hundreds of women whose young husbands or sons had vanished, I was struck by the patience and quiet strength that was a product of their devout nature. As Parveena Ahangar, still expecting to see her son fourteen years after he was picked up for interrogation, had said, 'Sabr.' Patience—it was Allah's will.

The young religious leader of Kashmir, Mirwaiz Umar Farooq, personally, remains a personable, dignified and likeable man of religion. His ancestral home isn't the typical maulvi sahib's home that one would see in other parts of the subcontinent. It is the modern-looking home of a scholar. His views on Islam are clear and mature. 'I strongly feel that imams should not be supported by the establishment,' he said. 'They should be supported by members of the community, and they should be professionals so that they keep in touch with the changing times.' He himself seemed to have done so. His daily routine changed with the requirements of the time. 'These days I am busy with my research project—the political thought of Islam with reference to Central Asia and Kashmir.' The confidence with which he spoke about his religious obligations seemed to run in some other homes of well-to-do Kashmiri Muslims that I visited. The former medical superintendent Dr Mir Nazir Ahmad— who retired in 1994 as the medical superintendent of the Shri Maharaja Hari Singh Medical College and who is the son of one of the close associates of Sheikh Abdullah, Mir Ghulam Rasool who had been arrested and imprisoned in the Kashmir Conspiracy Case—had, by his own admission, led a rather colourful life, complete with several women friends. Now he was a changed man, prayed five times a day and fasted the entire month of Ramzan. He even had plans to write a book on the revival of Islam. 'Earlier, I would spend the evenings at the Amar Singh Club or watch movies, but now it's either gardening or praying … today I call myself just a Muslim—no, don't add any prefix to it. I don't follow any leaders of the day; my leader is the Prophet of Islam.' His friends who were with us, an artist, a businessman and a professional gardener, all nodded in total agreement. They had all led different lives in the past, they said, but that was history. Each one of them held forth on the relevance of the teachings of Islam in the present-day scenario. And each told me how they had suffered humiliation in one way or the other in these last thirteen years, which directly changed their very perception of and approach to life. Dr Mir Nazir Ahmad had this to say: 'My house was cordoned off for a search at six on a winter morning. Jawans ordered me out and forced me to climb the hill outside the house, where I was made to sit on the ground till nine that night, guarded like a criminal. At one point my son tried to reason with them and one jawan pushed him down with the butt of his gun. Tell me, can I ever wipe out that humiliation? Is it really so difficult to conduct searches in a more humane manner?' Without his faith, he hinted, he would have come undone by now.

This was just a trading of the simple pleasures of life for the solace of religion, which was understandable—the loss of youth has done worse things to people. But what I found less appealing was the attitude of many young adults in Kashmir towards Islam and their co-religionists elsewhere. A surprisingly large number are aware of the happenings in the Arab world, and are uncritical of anything that is projected as a symbol of Muslim pride. Saddam Hussain, I was told over and over again, was a hero. What of all the cruelty he had unleashed on his own people? Surely, not everything about him was good? This made them indignant and it was made clear to me that I had been fooled by the propaganda of the West. A well-known young leader of a separatist group tried to temper this sentiment and sound reasonable: 'Saddam is a hero, and it isn't because he is a good Muslim but because he is the only Arab leader to have taken on the might of the US forces.' But then he betrayed his bias by concluding, 'You see, there is a great revival of the spirit of Islam today.' This meeting ended rather comically, with the young man, motivated, no doubt, by his Islamic sense of duty, gallantly proposing marriage to me after hearing about my recent separation. Diplomatically, I said to him that I was doing fine despite the separation, and also pointed out that he was almost the same age as my son. That did not seem relevant to him. 'When the Prophet married Khadija she was his senior by over twenty-two years, and yet he was so happy with her that during her lifetime he never married again. So we can be happy too. Give it a thought. I'm not going to hound you, but just try it out.' For some weeks after this adolescent proposal, I was extremely apprehensive, but true to his word the man never bothered me. If his orthodox sense of Islam ensured this much decency, despite the chauvinism, it was fine by me.

One sad result of the growing 'Arabization' of Islamic faith in the Valley is that the present generation of Kashmiris do not seem to attach much importance to the unique Sufi tradition of the Valley. Perhaps it would be best to describe Sufis in the words of the Mughal Emperor Jehangir (who, incidentally, referred to them as 'Muslim Rishis'):

> Though they ... have not religious knowledge or learning of any sort yet they possess simplicity and are without pretence. They abuse no one. They restrain the tongue of desire and the foot of seeking. They eat no flesh, they have no wives and always plant fruit-bearing trees in the fields so that men can benefit from them, themselves desiring no advantage.

Abu'l Fazl records his meeting with Sufi Wahid and it is said that he wrote to Emperor Akbar about the meeting:

> I met with the saint and the old sore of the divine longing opened afresh. For a long time he had lived like Uwais and Karkhi in a ruined habitation. He lived apart from joy and sorrow, and took nothing from anybody except

broken bread. Though I did not know the Kashmiri language yet I gathered much edification through an interpreter and a new vision dawned on me.

Such was the power of the Sufis. Yet today Kashmiris go looking for advice and solace and even for healing to religious men who are called 'pir sahibs' or simply 'pirs'. They are Muslim men who go wandering about from place to place, and even make predictions about the future. There's also the theory that several of them are Kashmiris who have been greatly disturbed by the violence around and have left their homes to wander about aimlessly, looking for peace.

The place of the Sufi saints seems to have been appropriated by these pirs. From the politicians of the day to middle-class Kashmiris with their mundane woes, tens of thousands seek their advice and intervention. In 2002, while I was staying at Butt's Clermont houseboats, the attendant, Ramzaana, insisted that I go along with him to his village in Gulmarg and visit the pir there. Why should I want to, I asked. But everybody must want something, he maintained. Besides, the pir of his village was popular with journalists—many came to see him, even from Delhi. 'One journalist, Sankarshan Thakur, comes here very often. Last year he went to ask pir sahib to bless him with a daughter and his wish was granted. And a French lady who was here last summer, she had some sort of cancer and he cured her ... and that friend of one ambassador sahib had problems with his wife and this pir sahib guided him so well that he got a divorce—just like that!' He went on, reeling off several other names and 'miracles'. The continuing turbulence of the last fourteen years has clearly left the local populace feeling emotionally disturbed and insecure. Hope is at a premium. So it is unsurprising that so many turn so easily to these pirs. Most of these pirs do not charge any fees, but it is true that each person who comes to them carries something in the form of an offering—a leg or a breast of a chicken, a bowl of rice, clothes, ornaments, plain currency.

Among the older lot, opinion is divided over these pirs. Most doctors, especially, frown at the growing influence of the pirs. A large number of the ill, especially those who are mentally disturbed, first go to these men and seek out doctors only when their condition has worsened and the case has become complicated. What are we supposed to do then, ask the doctors.

*

One of the most depressing changes in everyday Kashmiri life for a frequent visitor like me has been the passing away of the matter-of-fact grace and infectious joy in traditional Kashmiri families. Not a single family I met had happy memories of the recent past that they could share with me. Gone are the days when you could savour the warmth and general sense of well-being that came with spending time with a Kashmiri family—the refinement, the generosity, the comfort of ordinary household routine. Now you need nerves of steel to endure the sadness and the tension and to hear the horror stories that are so common.

This decay cuts across class barriers. Even in the sprawling residence of Abdul Ghani Lone's son Bilal, there is little mental peace despite the material comforts. Bilal said to me, 'Everybody is affected. It would be a lie to say we are leading normal lives. Blasts have taken place even on this road, at the end of this garden!' In sharp contrast to the Lone mansion was the little donga—a one-room wooden structure, a poor cousin of the houseboat—at one end of the Dal Lake where

Shareefa, the half widow lived in grim poverty with her three young children. She didn't need to say that life was not normal. The evidence was there to see. There was rarely enough food for them most days, and there was no man in the house to provide security. All Shareefa would do was 'wait'.

In Peer Bagh I visited the home of the slain activist lawyer Jaleel Andrabi. The house was full of people—Andrabi's three children, his widow Rifat and Andrabi's elder brother Arshad, whom Rifat had married—but it seemed empty of all spirit. Each face sagged under the weight of an unyielding burden. Rifat appeared briefly, then retreated to an inner room. Arshad, sitting with me in his dead brother's study, spoke for nearly ninety minutes, but not once did he look a shade less tense than when I had first entered the house. He recounted the turn of events. 'On 11 February 1984, after the execution of Maqbool Butt (founder of the Jammu and Kashmir National Liberation Front who was hanged in Delhi's Tihar Jail after the killing of an Indian diplomat), Jaleel had come out of the Bar and protested. He was arrested and lodged in the Hari Niwas interrogation centre in Srinagar. Though he was released after our house was searched and my father's licensed gun confiscated, he was a broken man. When the Hurriyat was formed in 1990 he was associated with it and in 1995 he was sent to Geneva as their representative for the UN's Human Rights Sub Commission. Thereafter, he visited USA and spoke so bluntly about the situation in the Valley that he was advised by many in the USA not to come back to India. But he came back, and he was hounded. First, on 26 January 1996, renegades sent by the forces came here but he managed to take their photographs and circulated them. Then on 7 March he was arrested and on 28 March 1996 he was found dead. Now the police say that the prime suspect in his murder is one Major Avtar Singh, who they say has committed nine other murders and today lives in Karnal, having been court-martialled by the army.' Arshad broke down at this point. When he had regained his composure, all he said was, 'There are thousands of Jaleel Andrabi type of cases, yet the official murderers move about freely ... what more can I say?' When I left that family, the despair and agony of their life together clung to me. What comfort could they offer each other?

I experienced the same helplessness in Dr Farida Ashai's official residence on the campus of the Bone and Joints Hospital. She told me of her husband Dr Farooq Ashai's murder as if it had happened just hours earlier. He had been shot dead before her eyes. 'The shots came from a particular bunker on the Barzullah Bridge. But no arrests were made. He was killed because he was an outspoken man who couldn't keep quiet about the condition of the patients who were brought to this hospital.' She spoke to me till late, sitting out on the lawns, as if unwilling to enter the four walls of her home with her memories.

What was most saddening was how the atmosphere of fear and suspicion had affected even the children. I was at the modest, middle-class home of the poet Zarif Ahmad Zarif, and he had just begun opening up to me—there was something he wanted to tell me, and just then his sad-eyed ten-year-old grandson mumbled that he shouldn't say anything. I was stunned by the barely audible request. What times were these, when a child had to look out for his grandfather? Zarif, looking defeated, was quiet after that. He would express himself in the coded language of his verse.

The Lost Generation

The last fourteen years must count as the most difficult time for the young in the history of Kashmir. Youth is a liability in times of strife, especially a separatist struggle: it makes you extra visible, the favourite target of militant outfits in constant need of new recruits and the security forces under constant pressure to show results in their battle against insurgency. Neutrality is hardly ever an option, and whichever side you are on, you must pay the price for making a choice.

But it is a fact that while a young Kashmiri can be reasonably certain of what not to do in order to avoid the wrath of the militants—who can be brutal with anyone suspected of being an 'informer'—they can never be sure with the security forces. There is a bungalow on Gupkar Road, known till not so long ago as Papa 11, that served as an interrogation centre in Srinagar. Even hardened militants have cringed when recalling what went on there. For a long time, young men in Kashmir lived in terror of one day finding themselves in Papa 11, because there was never any way of predicting what provoked the security forces to pick up people and take them away for interrogation. The actions of the forces are still arbitrary, but at least Papa 11 does not exist any more—a few years ago it was converted, astonishingly, into the official residence for a senior bureaucrat, Ashok Jaitly, considered close to Farooq Abdullah, and is now occupied by Muzaffar Baigh, minister for finance and law in the Mufti Mohammad Sayeed government.

But interrogations clearly did not stop after Papa 11 was shut down. The situation continues to be bad in rural Kashmir. In the autumn of 2002 I had witnessed the absolute despair of the cook at the Raj Bagh guest house whose son had been picked up from his village in Tanmarg by the security forces. The boy was eventually released, but had been beaten so severely that he couldn't be driven to a hospital in town. The teenaged waiters who had gathered around the cook, trying to console him, later told me that they had all been packed off from their villages by their families so that they would escape the wrath of the security forces, because either they themselves or some relative had been roughed up. One waiter, I remember, had become almost hysterical describing the time his blind brother was picked up and forced to state 'what his sightless eyes had seen'.

In Srinagar, not just the rich but even several of my friends who were of the middle class had employed at least a couple of young servant boys. 'We haven't a choice,' one of my friends told me. 'Their parents want them out of the villages and they have nowhere they can stay in the city. We can't just turn them all away.' The belief is that urban areas are relatively safer. 'They [the parents] feel their sons are better off here, away from the lure of militancy and the excesses of the security forces. Our boys are trapped—they are being targeted from both sides.'

I asked several parents with young sons, in Srinagar and in the surrounding villages, whether they feared the security forces more or the militant outfits. The answer was invariably the same: they were more afraid of the boys being 'dragged away to be interrogated'. Most likely, the parents said, they would never come back, or if they did come back alive, they would be 'deranged because of the torture'. One parent even told me about boys whose 'private parts had been rendered *bekaar* [useless]'. What about the militants, I asked. What if militants barged in to drag their sons away to join some group that spread terror in the name of religion? What if the boys were forced to work for the ISI? Didn't that scare them? Most parents shook their heads vigorously, clearly disturbed by the question. Not many would want to say anything further. The few who did, would say nothing specifically about the militants. About Pakistan, they were clear: 'No, we have nothing to do with Pakistan. There was that stage in the early 1990s when Pakistan was seen as a saviour by even our professors and doctor sahibs, not just our boys ... but not today. We've seen through [Pakistan's] games ... Actually, everybody wants to eat us alive, from China to America to Pakistan to the *hukumat* [government] here! We just want to be left in peace!'

There have been reports of jehadi groups operating in Kashmir, but with headquarters outside the Valley, terrorizing locals in the rural districts. But for fear, people rarely talk about this on record. It is the more frequent callousness and brutality of divisions of the security forces, especially towards young men, that they are most vocal about—and rightly so; no one expects terrorist groups to have any respect for the law or for human rights. Unfortunately, it has become routine for even senior ministers in the NDA government at the Centre to counter any mention of human rights abuse by the army with the question: 'What about the human rights of the innocents killed by terrorists?' My hope is that someone in the army, at least, will realize what this kind of response implies, and object.

The 2002 elections in Kashmir gave me the opportunity

to move beyond Srinagar city. As I travelled with fellow
reporters and news photographers to the interiors of Pulwama
district, many young men pleaded that we should stay there
longer, pointing at the armed Rashtriya Rifles men going
inside homes. With journalists around, the men felt safer. In
Shopian town we saw several uniformed men going in and
out of almost every house we could see. When we asked their
officer about this, he said these were routine searches. But a
number of agitated young men we met soon afterwards told
us—almost shrieking in helpless rage and fear—that they were
being pulled out and threatened that once we media people
moved on, they would be taught the lesson of their lives.
This was the pattern in most of the villages and small towns
we travelled through. Insecurity and fear loomed large. The
most telling episode was, again, in Shopian. I saw a group of
teenaged boys standing huddled by the side of the main
market and requested one of the RR men if he would stand
next to them for a photograph. He agreed, but no sooner
had he got close to the boys than they shuffled away and
stood in a tighter huddle, almost trembling in fright. It took
the uniformed soldier some time to convince them that he
meant no harm. After I had taken the picture, I pointed out
their reaction to the RR man. He smiled sheepishly and said
that at least he and his men had never harassed a single person;
the boys reminded him of his own children back home in
Punjab; why would he harm them?

   That man had seemed sincere enough, but a couple of
days later, I visited a friend's orchards in village Romo that
lies off the Pulwama–Shopian road, and met the commanding
officer of a BSF company stationed there who turned out to
be the worst kind of advertisement for the armed forces in
Kashmir. His demeanour, even the way he walked and the
tone he used when talking to the locals, was designed to

intimidate people. With absolute confidence he told me that yes, tough measures were used with the youth, 'even with those who are picked up on grounds of suspicion'. He made no bones about this; to achieve any kind or result, he said, it was necessary.

Every issue of *Missive* gives details of custodial deaths, killings, rapes and disappearances in the Valley, the perpetrators named being not just from the security forces but also militant outfits and renegades (and even the Pakistani army which resorts to unprovoked shelling and firing from across the LOC). The victims are not all Muslims, but they are almost always young and in most cases residents of rural Kashmir. As a senior correspondent stationed in Srinagar put it, 'The complexion of the turmoil has changed—the focus has shifted to the interiors.' Senior psychiatrists confirm that a large number of their patients in recent years come from the villages and small towns of the Valley and that they are mostly women and young men.

*

Security for the young is a concern for every Kashmiri family. Upper-middle-class families pack their sons off to colleges and technical institutes in cities like Delhi and Bangalore, Jammu and Chandigarh, and some even to the smaller towns of western UP and Uttaranchal. Mumbai and Ahmedabad were on the list too, but after the Mumbai riots of 1992 and the post-Godhra communal killings in Gujarat, few Kashmiri Muslims consider either city safe. Faculty members of at least two Srinagar colleges told me that when there was a plan, recently, to send NCC cadets from Srinagar to Gujarat, parents put their foot down, insisting that they wouldn't risk their children going to 'Modi's Gujarat'. Tariq Mir, a young staffer with the *Indian Express*, had the enthusiasm to venture as far as Mumbai for his job after passing out of university, and he enjoyed the job too. But the enthusiasm soured in March 2002. Midway into the rioting in Gujarat, his landlord asked him to vacate the flat as other residents of the Gujarati-majority apartment building did not want a Muslim, especially one from Kashmir, among them.

The attacks on the Parliament and the Akshardham temple, with images being telecast mindlessly, over and over again, on television channels, have instilled fear and easy hatred in the minds of a majority of Indians. And since neither the government nor the television channels made any effort to distinguish the terrorists responsible for these attacks from ordinary Kashmiris, it isn't surprising that not many people outside the Valley want to have anything to do with Kashmiris, and see nothing wrong when the authorities persecute them. In the first two months of 2003, Kashmiri youth were picked up by the police in Maharashtra and Uttar Pradesh. If the print media hadn't highlighted these incidents, few would have heard of them, and there wouldn't have been even a murmur of protest. Some of the boys who were picked up were from families of modest means who had sold precious land to send their sons out of the Valley so they would escape the violence. But cases like the arrest of two Kashmiri students in Uttar Pradesh, on charges of being Jaish-e-Mohammed activists, proved to them that nowhere in India could they expect any security. The two agriculture students—Ajaz Husain Jan and Mehrajuddin Shaikh, both Kashmiris and both in their final year of BSc—were picked up from the Rashtriya Kisan Post Graduate College in small-town Shamli. The Chief Minister Mufti Mohammad Sayeed and the president of the National Conference Omar Abdullah described it as a witch-hunt and took the matter up with the

Centre and the UP government. When police officers in Kashmir (not Muslims, incidentally—things have deteriorated so much that this needs to be said) cross-checked the students' credentials, they found nothing to suggest links with any militant group. But will it always take intervention by chief ministers and home ministers for justice to be done—or rather, for injustice to be undone? This is the question many from the Valley ask. In UP alone, students in Meerut and Ghaziabad are routinely questioned and threatened and live in constant fear of the police. What if news of their arrest doesn't get to the media? What if newspapers have more momentous things to cover and can't be bothered? Why should an entire generation have to live with such fear and humiliation?

Over the past three or four years, there have been reports of Kashmiri students being harassed and discriminated against even in the capital. So families who can afford it send their boys abroad. The leading paediatrician of the Valley Dr Altaf Hussain decided, after the Gujarat riots, to send his son to Malaysia for further studies. Why not Delhi or Bangalore, I asked. 'I don't find any place in the country safe any more,' he replied. And Srinagar, his home, was the least safe of all: 'My neighbour's fifteen-year-old son Farooq, whom I'd been treating for a serious illness, is untraceable. Strange things are happening in this city and all this calm that you see is deceptive.' So the doctor was forced to think of Malaysia, an Islamic country, as a temporary home for his own son. Several other parents I met in Srinagar had sent their sons to Iran for medical studies. 'Because in Iran,' they explained, 'you are taught much more than academics ... they teach you Islamic culture, and unlike in the US, your kids are not drawn away from you, they return. And don't forget, we Kashmiris are of Central Asian stock.'

The Indian government's mishandling of the situation in Kashmir has displaced not just the Pandits but also large numbers of younger Kashmiri Muslims. Who would have thought they would seek refuge in Malaysia and Iran? And the flight will continue. There are no exact figures available for the number of Kashmiri students studying in New Delhi, but from the PUDR findings and also from my own interactions with the students, it is clear that most of them face a certain degree of humiliation in the city and live in unease and insecurity. A couple of years back, a senior reader in the department of geography at the Jamia Millia University, Dr Haseena Hashia, told me that students coming from the Valley find it difficult to get a room on rent and often she ends up keeping several of them in her own home. A young woman from Srinagar, working as a reporter in the Capital, confided that on Eid that year she was aware of her neighbours in south Delhi keeping an eye on her because she had more than the usual share of visitors coming to see her. In the first week of January 2002, a Kashmiri student, twenty-three-year-old Zaffer Iqbal, had been found dead in south Delhi. The details of the case unearthed and published by *Missive* in its January 2002 issue seemed to suggest that it was a custodial death. I asked the young reporter for her comments on the incident, but she refused. 'No Kashmiri will speak on this incident,' she said, 'because the police will get after them. We want to live here in total anonymity ... you announce your Kashmiri Muslim identity and problems begin.'

Another young journalist I interviewed was Srinagar-based Naseer Ahmad, a gold medallist of the Media Education Research Centre (MERC) of Kashmir University who had earlier worked with the *Kashmir Monitor* till it was shut down due to financial constraints. His shift to Delhi had brought him little relief. 'I did my internship from the *Times of India* but after that there was no job available in that newspaper or in any other. Living in New Delhi was tough—a Sikh gentleman provided me free boarding in Jhilmil Colony, but I could sense the neighbours watching my every move. And the fact that I was unemployed made it worse—what was I supposed to do ... beg for a job? I decided to return, although even here I'm sitting jobless. My father runs a shop and I'm dependent on him.' Another Kashmir University student, Mohammad Asif, told me that he had also tried his luck working in New Delhi, but he had lasted there for only twenty days. Why? 'I didn't feel comfortable. The moment even a passer-by heard the word "Kashmiri", he'd look at me as though I was a terrorist ... I wasn't called an *atankwadi* to my face, but the body language, the manner in which they spoke to me made it quite clear that I was unwanted.' Back home, in Srinagar's Dal Gate locality, the going is tough again. 'I've had pretty bad experiences during the crackdowns ... only recently an officer-rank army guy slapped me around because I was not walking in a line along with the rest of the men during a search operation. Of course Kashmiris are alienated and this sense of alienation will never go away—after all this third-class treatment how can you expect it to? The damage has been done. Since 1990 we've lost over a lakh of lives ... there can be no going back.'

When men and students from the Valley go to New Delhi, the ordeal of trying to find a place in a lodge or guest house or a room on rent is not the only humiliation they experience. They are also required to visit the local police station and give details of their visit together with their names and addresses. Those worst affected by this are the Kashmiri workers and vendors. A couple of affluent businessmen of New Delhi gave me graphic accounts of how the young Kashmiri workers they employed were harassed by the police, but they pleaded that I shouldn't quote them—'we might have to shut down otherwise!'

*

Not all the young people in the Valley live in numbing despair or want to leave for other places in India or across the border. In fact, it might sound strange, even ironical, but each time I have felt out of sorts in Delhi, I have made it a point to travel to Srinagar because you will find a number of people there, many of them young, making things work for themselves and for others in spite of the enormous odds against them. And your own problems seem too puny in comparison.

My first encounters with young Kashmiri men on each trip to the Valley have happened in auto-rickshaws, driving from the airport to the hotel, and from there to different locations in Srinagar for interviews. The drivers are almost all in their twenties or thirties. As their autos bump along possibly the worst maintained roads in India, and after they are convinced that I can be trusted and are at ease with me, they talk endlessly. They tell me all about themselves, their names, their problems, their dreams and disappointments— some of them sad-eyed and looking vaguely lost, and others like excitable young boys, vulnerable one minute and full of bravado the next. It is a wonder I haven't fallen in love with any of them. As a visitor in Kashmir, surrounded by so much beauty and sadness and listening to moving accounts of traumatized lives, you are always in danger of that sort of thing. I remember one driver, thirty-year-old Basheer Ahmad, a man with gentle eyes and a soft voice, telling me about the harrowing experiences of his life and the psyche of young Kashmiri men like him. When I asked about his family, his wife and children, he braked abruptly. 'Family! Of course not! I've decided not to marry—how can I? I am a graduate but I can barely feed myself ... who will feed the extra mouths? I have seen so much of violence and tragedy ... my father is dead, my mother has been ill for years, my younger brother does nothing. I can think of nothing but our survival. When I was in college I did think of marriage and women, but not now ... these years have changed me, ruined us all—whether it is the Pandits who had to run away or we who remain in this strange city where even the dead are guarded [an obvious reference to Sheikh Abdullah's grave that is guarded round the clock] ...'

During my visits to the Valley in 2002, I didn't travel very much by autos, having graduated by then to hopping onto buses, which was a good way to chat with students. One of the few times I took an auto, the driver turned out to be a school dropout who looked like an improved version of Aamir Khan but seemed least interested in what Bollywood was churning out. All that didn't interest him, he said, and in any case, where would he get to see films on the big screen. 'Which theatre can one go to? Those two—Neelam and Broadway—they are only meant for the sarkari rich who can pay hundred, two hundred for a ticket. But why go there—in this city a theatre is enacted every day by the government agencies.' Their lies, he said, sickened him.

Others I met, though equally angry, try to do something positive. Khurram Parvez, a young student at the MERC, helps his activist uncle Parvez Imroz run the APDP, and in spite of trouble with the establishment, he seems in no mood to give up the struggle. Khurram and his colleague took several hours out of their hectic schedule and accompanied me to the homes of the mothers and wives of 'disappeared' men. The APDP office has been attacked and Parvez Imroz even had to move out of Srinagar for several months. But none of that has deterred Khurram. 'I have two brothers,' he said, 'so even if I'm killed my parents will have two sons with them.'

Gowher Fazili, an environmentalist turned teacher, also refuses to let the violence and chaos in the Valley undermine his determination to work for a better life for his people. When I first met him he worked for Green Kashmir, a movement to save the dying Dal Lake. He told me about his work, sitting in his office inside a compact donga on Nageen Lake. 'When all this trouble began here, I was in my late teens. I saw so much torture of civilians that I reached a stage that was beyond anger. I really don't know how to explain it, but once you are exposed to too much pain you react in a different way. I wanted to work from a platform that would allow me to contribute to people's lives effectively, and this project with its focus on saving the Dal seemed ideal, given how much our lives depend on the lake. Caught up in the everyday turmoil, none of us really thought about it. It was Charles Goschen, a British tourist, who drew our attention about six years back to the sorry state of the Dal—it was dying, due to the polluting waste being dumped into it. Charles decided to stay on, learnt the local language and began the Green Kashmir Movement. He didn't make any fancy speeches—he was a hands-on person, helping the boatman actually lift the garbage. That was what drew me to his cause. Charles died some time ago in a swimming accident while on a visit to South Africa, but his movement continues.'

Perhaps the movement is still as strong, but Fazili has started working for other causes as well; he is also involved now in a youth-related project. It was through him that I met a young volunteer translator attached to a foreign organization who had a lot to say about human rights violations taking place in the Valley. But he made it quite clear that he couldn't be quoted—'That's because of my work regulations ... but you will see for yourself.' And as I travelled in and around Srinagar I did notice that all the young people I met looked depressed and prematurely aged. At the MERC, where I was speaking on the subject of reporting from a region in conflict, one of the faculty members came up to me and asked whether I remembered him. 'I'm Nasir Mirza,' he said, 'we met in 1985 when my batch, the first batch of this course, was visiting New Delhi.' I nodded politely, but it was hours later that I finally placed him. The twenty-something student had in barely seventeen years become haggard and middle-aged. The students I addressed that day were a far cry from their counterparts in Delhi or Bombay, the confident, comfortable mainstream Indian youth who tend to be aggressive and fashionably turned out. These students looked worried and tense—apprehensive about their future. One student, Mohammad Ali Tak, said to me, 'Every month my family spends at least 3000 rupees on my lodging and boarding, but I'm not sure what I will do after this course is over ... jobs are very difficult to get.' He spoke with such innocence that it was impossible not to be affected by his anxiety and bewilderment. According to Justice A.S. Anand, the basic problem related to the turmoil centres around this factor alone: 'Frustration amongst the young is immense, and mainly due to growing unemployment, otherwise Kashmiri Muslims were never known to be violent.'

That afternoon, few students spoke during the question-answer session. Among the few who did were two students who had begun working as trainee reporters for *Amar Ujjala* and *Dainik Bhaskar*, and they hinted that in most magazines and newspapers young reporters had little freedom. I had been told this by other journalists too, that their copy was often changed drastically and they had no say in the matter.

Another student, Shaiq Nazir, disillusioned by the lack of opportunities and freedom, had decided to concentrate instead on running an educational trust for orphans in Srinagar's Batamaloo locality. Abdul Mohaimin had found no such enterprise to handle his frustration—'I have so many ideas on what to write, but I'm confused and in the end can't manage to write at all.' Describing his mental state, Peerzada Arshad said that his mind was 'in hibernation'. It was depressing to hear many an earnest-looking student say that he or she regularly sent articles or letters about living in the midst of so much turmoil to several newspapers, but nothing ever got published. They sought some sort of release, but there was none.

Almost every tenth youngster in Srinagar has taken to putting his or her feelings down on paper. Even students living on zero budget pour their emotions out on pieces of paper. It is therapeutic. Some of it gets published, but only in modest periodicals. A surprising number of periodicals and small-budget newspapers have been started over the last decade or so, and several of these have actually managed to survive. Noorul Qamraan, the young editor of the weekly *Muslim Kashmir*, says, 'Most people, for obvious reasons, prefer a secure job, but I started out on my own for reasons pertaining to independence in writing, which definitely means editorial independence. The going's tough, but one has to pay the price for writing fearlessly.' But not everyone can keep afloat. Some of the literary set-ups, especially, are shutting down. At Bilal Lone's home I met one of his party's key workers, thirty-year-old Mohammad Aslam Bhat, who told me that he had had to wind up his journal, even quit his job with the daily *Subeh Kashmir*, and start a more secure venture—a news agency called Kashmir News Service.

I have met many youngsters who write poems by the dozen

every week, but few can afford to have volumes of their work published—it can be done for a fee. Others write on chits and scraps of paper and never bother to put the verses together. A law student, Shafaat Naseem, told me that he wrote his poems only on loose sheets which he left lying around anywhere; he couldn't be bothered. But didn't he feel there was some value attached to the written word? 'No longer,' he said. 'When you aren't sure what will become of you the next hour, what value can words have?'

Faith, on the other hand, appears to have greater value. Under siege, the Kashmiri youth seek security in Muslim identity—one that binds them to the larger, global Muslim community. In all the years that I've been travelling to Kashmir, I haven't seen as many young people throng the mosque for Friday prayers than in the past few years. One evening in late 2002, I visited a particular newspaper bureau which is manned by seven to eight young, educated, English-speaking men. I walked into a heated argument between the young boss and his staffers. After a couple of minutes it became clear that the boss had fallen in love with a non-Muslim and was inclined to marry her, and his staffers were bitterly opposed to this. 'You cannot marry a non-Muslim,' one of them fumed. 'After all this ... after the Gujarat massacre, how can you even think of marrying a Hindu!' Then they turned on me: how could I, after Gujarat, let down the community by accepting the prospect of a Hindu daughter-in-law? (They knew that my son had a close lady friend who was a Rajput.) I was taken aback, and could only mumble something about love being God's gift and mere humans shouldn't interfere, which remark was greeted with sniggers.

*

In Srinagar, there are few opportunities for recreation. Not only are the movie theatres too expensive for most young people, going to these is hardly a pleasant experience, given that cops keep an eye on every move and the more regressive of the militant groups frown at such 'un-Islamic' activities. The only operational club is the Amar Singh Club, accessible only to a select few. Snooker parlours have come up but are strictly for men, and only a small percentage can afford them anyway. The three golf courses are again for the chosen lot, with one reserved exclusively for the police. Till mid-2003, cellphones, the new toys of the young elsewhere, were banned in the Valley (the only effect this had was of alienating Kashmiris further; it made little difference to the militants whose satellite phones worked well enough for them). Internet connections are still difficult to get.

Life comes to a standstill even before dusk. Even during the day there isn't much to do. Simple romance, too, isn't easy. Young boys and girls find it impossible to spend time together. Many teenaged boys from affluent families complained that they had steady girlfriends but could not go out with them. The city is like a place under occupation, anyway, they say, with tanks and checkpoints and soldiers with guns everywhere. And if you go looking for a secluded spot, you are being suspicious and asking for trouble. Few restaurants have private cubicles where they can sit and talk in peace. So what do they do? How many aimless auto rides can they take, just to be together, undisturbed?

I remember the time the auto driver Basheer took me to the ziarat of the Iraqi Sufi Dastgeer Sahib and then to the adjoining one of Yousef Aza. He parked his vehicle at some safe spot and accompanied me to the shrine, talking non-stop till one of the caretakers had to intervene. They had a brief exchange in Kashmiri, which ended when the caretaker shook his head and said something fiercely that made Basheer blush. He was awkward and silent for a while after that. I asked him what the caretaker had said, but he was evasive. When I persisted, he mumbled, 'These days most young people have nowhere to take their loved ones, so they go around in autos or come to ziarats to sit and talk. That mad man thought I'd brought you here to ... er ... talk, you know. I told him that you are like my sister but he said this excuse is beginning to get too common!'

Some hotel and restaurant owners confirmed that young people have a tough time. One of them accused the cops: '*Policewale bahut tang karte hain* [the policemen harass them] ... they want money if they spot a young pair on the Boulevard. There is no freedom here.' The girls are the worst affected because they suffer the added restrictions imposed by their families, since the disturbance has hardened conservative attitudes. A young Sikh businessman based in the Valley said to me once, 'The level of frustration among the girls is almost pathetic. For one, parents don't allow them to move out, and then even if they have a friend, where do they go? When I go driving in my Maruti I find so many girls wanting a lift!'

When I visited Srinagar's College for Women on Maulana Azad Road, two severe-looking chowkidars armed with lathis stood at the gate to keep the girls in and any visitors out. Short of using their lathis, they did everything they could to shoo me away to one end of the road where I had to wait till one of the teachers came to escort me in. Agitated, I protested to the faculty about this barbaric method of controlling the girls. Some of the senior faculty members justified it, saying, 'You can't imagine what these years have done to the new generation. Because of the crackdowns and curfews most were not allowed to leave home; now it is as though each one of them wants to make up for those years. But there's nowhere that they can go even for an outing—all the usual places, including Chashme Shahi, Gulmarg, Pahalgam, have been taken up by the army.' But the girls were getting rebellious, one professor said, and this was worrying—'How long can we make them sit indoors!'

The Kashmir University campus is the best place to see how the normal pattern of young lives—romance, activism, idealism, camaraderie—has been affected. It wasn't easy getting into the campus; the vice chancellor had made it clear that journalists were not welcome. In fact, after NDTV's Barkha Dutt interviewed some students on the campus shortly before my visit—and the whole country heard some radical stuff from them on TV—he had imposed an unofficial ban on the entry of anyone from her tribe. So each time I entered the sprawling campus, I posed as a conservative woman— since this allowed me to cover much of my face with my dupatta—who had failed several times but was determined to get a degree. On none of these visits did I spot more than three or four couples in secluded corners of the campus. Mostly, students walked about in groups but the atmosphere was unnaturally subdued—unnatural because you would normally expect noise and variety and some life in a university campus with over three thousand students. I only sensed disquiet. A former faculty member had told me to watch out for this. He had been shocked himself by the change—during his time, he had said, in the 1970s and 1980s, the place had been like any other university. There was romance and student politics and cultural activities. Now it was as if such things were irrelevant, even trivial, and the students and professors all looked cowed down or grim.

There is no students union in the university. Crackdowns by the security forces are routine in the campus; even staff quarters are searched and night detentions take place. A BSF unit is stationed on the campus—it has occupied the guest house—and militants also move around in it. Without wanting to be quoted, several students said to me, 'We are caught between the two ... it's a strange situation we are facing yet we can't even speak out.' Even the vice chancellor didn't want to speak on the issue; his personal assistant made sure I didn't reach him.

It was outside the university, on Residency Road and its many offshoots, that I had some success with the young men manning the shops there. A surprisingly large percentage of them were educated, articulate people. It was as though they had decided to fight back by doing the best they could to survive against the odds, and that gave them the courage to speak out, unlike the students in the university who were unwilling to jeopardize their careers.

Meanwhile, young Indians outside the Valley are oblivious to what is happening there. Speaking at Aligarh Muslim University's Kennedy Hall in early 2003, I asked the students who were doing their masters in human rights why they never thought of going to the Valley and interacting with Kashmiri students. They had no answer. Even the youth bodies of the main opposition political parties like the Congress, CPI and CPI (M) are not bothered; their rallies never reach Kashmir. It is left to human rights activists like Gautam Navlakha and his colleague Vijay, counsellors and personnel from the Rajiv Gandhi Foundation, and journalists to try and bring us the truth or work towards some positive interventions in the troubled region. The activists and journalists, of course, have the odds stacked against them. The former are attacked for being partisan, self-serving liberals married to every terrorist's cause. And the latter, too, have their credibility questioned at every stage—the young journalist and writer David Devdas, who has been living in the Valley for months, told me that when he had gone to interview the intelligence top brass with some hard facts on his fingertips, one of the men snapped, 'You know all the facts! Has the ISI equipped you with them?'

So the gap between Kashmir and the rest of India continues to widen. It was pathetic to hear even the kids of the who's who in the Valley ask rather naively, '*Aapki Dilli mein yeh hota hai*? [Does this happen in your Delhi],' referring to any bit of news they had heard about life in the capital. It wasn't much different from our wide-eyed grand-aunts in the 1950s and 1960s asking about life in America or Australia. Young people elsewhere in the country, of course, do not show any such curiosity about Kashmir. To them Kashmir is a place of terror, and a paradise where they should be able to travel but cannot because of unreasonable, pro-Pakistan insurgents. They neither know nor care about the rich culture of the Valley—its music, poetry, spiritual traditions. And yet, they are certain that Kashmir is and must remain an 'integral part of India'. They will not put pressure on their government to be more humane, to take concrete efforts to lessen the humiliation that the Kashmiris experience every day. I am dismayed by the self-absorption of our youth. Even among the small percentage who are sensitive to the sufferings of others, most are more easily moved by the state of orphans in Africa than in Kashmir. Not their fault entirely. How many of them get to hear of the grim reality in the Valley? I quote from a report that appeared in the January 2002 issue of *Missive*:

Children constitute 38% of J&K state's population. Out of these, 5–6% are either orphans or destitute, neglected ones who do not get basic needs fulfilled in the present turmoil ... Due to the increasing number of orphans in the state, one has to think of the rights, protection and liberties of orphans ... The orphanages run by NGOs and other agencies have also been raided by the security forces ... thousands of orphans have been exploited by their relatives ...

I could go on and on describing cases where the young are the worst sufferers, and yet there is no platform for them to seek help or redress. The pages of *Missive* and similar journals are full of such stories. I'll mention just two that have affected me the most: The last time I was in Srinagar, I was told of a young girl, barely in her teens, who was booked under the draconian Prevention of Terrorism Act (POTA) because her boyfriend was involved in some militant activity, and though she pleaded her innocence—saying that she was not aware of his activities—she was arrested and charged under POTA. Shortly before this, in June 2002, a seventeen-year-old girl from Baramulla had been booked under the Public Safety Act (PSA). She had pleaded in a letter from the central jail where she was lodged that she had been implicated by a Special Task Force personnel, but there was no relief for her.

There are several hundred such cases of possibly innocent youngsters locked up in jail without being given a chance to be heard. There are thousands of others who live in fear of such a fate. This is the generation of whom we expect an unequivocal commitment to India.

Scenes from an Election

I don't know whether it is a good thing to travel around in a state during elections. With things in a state of flux, so to speak, you can hear and see things that you ordinarily might not. Yet, while the electorate are usually in their element at election time, they are not always so in a disturbed state. Also, with the entire official machinery geared towards polling bandobasts, there is little you will see of how they respond— or don't—to everyday realities. Politicians, generally not known to be categorical or consistent, are even more circumspect and propagandist during polls, and the bureaucrats, of course, are at their wits' end and prefer not to deal with any file or say anything significant on record— after all, they aren't sure who their next boss will be.

Interestingly, while in other states of the country it is the bureaucracy which is wary of journalists during polls, in Kashmir the scenario seemed quite the opposite. One afternoon, I was in the office of the chief of the Srinagar bureau of a national daily when he got a call. He sounded pretty agitated while talking on the phone. After he had slammed the receiver down, he explained that the call was from a police officer who had been transferred overnight from the north Kashmir district of Lolab where re-polling had been ordered after a NC candidate was shot dead. The officer, apparently, was angry with the bureau chief, saying that it was the report in his newspaper which was responsible for the transfer orders. Several other media persons told me that during polling they had had to brave not just the diktats of the militants but also the subtle and not so subtle telephonic warnings from high-ranking officials, some of whom, they said, 'were behaving like viceroys from the bygone era'.

In the streets of Srinagar, a majority of the people I spoke to were vocal about their decision not to vote. The Hurriyat men had made it amply clear that as far as they were concerned the elections were meaningless; Mirwaiz Umar Farooq's rationale was, 'We have had eight elections but the Kashmir crisis continues, so what good are they?' The middle class of the city echoed the Hurriyat sentiment. What if they were forced to vote by the government, I asked. They still wouldn't, they told me. One young shopkeeper said with childlike glee, 'In the last elections there was coercion—the army entered our home, looking for male members of the family. But I managed to sneak out!' Besides, many of them acknowledged that it was unlikely they would be forced as on previous occasions—that harsh reality was now to be seen in rural Kashmir, not in Srinagar. And what if they were coerced by various militant organizations not to vote, even if they wanted to? But why would that happen, they said, it was their own decision not to vote, no one needed to thrust it upon them.

What surprised me was that it was the so-called educated urban lot who seemed very clear about the decision to boycott the elections—people like B.A. Dabla, head of the sociology department of Kashmir University, the former Fulbright fellowship holder Agha Ashraf, the Kashmir University Teachers Association president Bashir Ahmad, and several other professors and professionals. Even before I could put the question to them, they would sense what was coming and start shaking their heads. There were a few, mostly the spouses of the rich and powerful, who were not entirely sure, or so they said, and remained non-committal: 'We haven't decided ... we will at the last minute.'

There were only a handful of people who seemed to think it worth their while to vote just so the civic problems could be resolved, if nothing else. They had their spokesperson in Taj Mohiuddin, the Congressman from Uri and son of the freedom fighter Brigadier Khuda Baksh. Sitting in one of the rooms of the Hotel Broadway, he argued forcefully, 'What does this no-voting concept mean? It's sheer nonsense. Suppose there's no azadi for fifty years—does that mean there should be no one to look after your civic structure? No, I'm not crying for independence here; people in my region only want to live in peace and dignity.'

Looking back, it is impossible to say just what percentage of Srinagar's electorate voted, and if civic problems were a factor at all. What was clear was the anti-National Conference mood. I witnessed a NC rally at Hazratbal, close to where Sheikh Abdullah's remains lie, guarded round the clock. There was no enthusiasm at all among the shoppers and shopkeepers along the route. 'Have you also come in an imported car?' a student asked me. 'These NC people move about only in foreign cars. I've seen their big cars on these roads, but this is the first time I'm seeing their faces.' And then he turned away, as did most of the others, to watch several middle-aged women singing and dancing in a marriage procession. Unlike the politicians, these women, to them, were an integral part of society. Bored with the rally, I too sat on the green stretch by the Dal Lake and watched the traditional Kashmiri marriage dance. After a while, a group of college girls came up to me and asked what I was doing with a pen and diary. When I told them, they were openly inquisitive and asked the most basic questions about politics and politicians in New Delhi, as if the capital was in another continent. We spoke for close to an hour. Finally, their parting query left me stumped: 'Is it true that Omar Abdullah's wife has been planted here by a foreign agency?' they asked. 'After all, she's a non-Muslim and she hasn't even allowed circumcision to be performed on her sons ... and she has taken over some airline office here.' This last was later confirmed by the staff of Destination Tours. Payal Abdullah is indeed the General Sales Agent (GSA) of Jet Airlines, nicknamed Kashmir Airlines since most in the government flew by Jet. To all the other reasons for the NC's unpopularity, ranging from Farooq Abdullah's flip-flop politics and luxurious lifestyle to rumours of massive corruption among the NC MLAs, had been added another— Payal Abdullah. If this was the level of disillusionment with the Abdullahs, where people were finding fault with just about everything to do with the family, it seemed clear to me that in case the elections did conclude without any major incident or any interference from the authorities, the NC government would be out.

Meanwhile, the bluff and bluster, the cajoling, the promises and inducements that usually mark electioneering seemed to be absent in Srinagar. I went about asking different associations and apolitical bodies whether they had been approached by any of the politicians or party workers and the answer was a clear no. The APDP lawyers said that no politician had approached them. The head of the Fishermen's Association told me exactly the same thing, as did the Weavers Association and members of several teachers' bodies. This seemed a strange kind of election. There could be only one plausible explanation: people's unwillingness to vote had been so clearly relayed to the politicians that they probably thought it would be a useless exercise trying to build any pro-election mood in Srinagar.

I was also struck by the near absence of any politician from New Delhi or other parts of the country. There were some familiar faces from the Congress in the Valley, but no one else. The BJP and other Sangh Parivar firebrands ventured only as far as Jammu. Even the so-called defenders of the minority groups in UP and Bihar and MP—Mulayam Singh, Amar Singh, Laloo Yadav, Mayawati, Kanshi Ram—were not to be seen. Their space, interestingly, seemed to have been taken over by the television reporters. They descended on Srinagar with their cameras and confidence and made sure that their presence was noticed. Most young people in Srinagar seemed to recognize the 'Star girls'. Boring print journalists like me had to acknowledge the power of television and eat humble pie! I remember the time we were talking to a well-known member of the administration in Srinagar and he seemed quite distracted during the interview, till he finally stopped talking midway. 'Oh, I'd better rush, Maya is waiting.' Mayawati? How come we hadn't heard of her arrival? But it turned out that he was referring to Maya Mirchandani, the popular NDTV reporter.

*

The indications were positive for a fair poll. The Election Commission, headed by the Chief Election Commissioner J.M. Lyngdoh, had inspired confidence in us hacks, at least. The foreign media had been allowed into the state to cover the elections. Envoys of various European countries were present as observers. (They were lodged in a leading hotel in Srinagar, but there was no apparent curiosity about them amongst the locals, though some did wonder why there were no observers from Muslim or Middle Eastern countries. In any case, none of the envoys were moving about independently; a great majority of them were either put in helicopters or in government cars and it was just a handful who brushed aside security to move about and see the situation for themselves.)

Leading up to polling day in Srinagar, 1 October, there were no major untoward incidents, yet most people preferred not to step out. Schools and colleges remained closed for days prior to polling. One school principal confided that they couldn't take any chances, given that shoot-outs had happened in the past even on normal days. Polling day itself was observed more like a holiday, with most families remaining indoors, not even venturing out into their gardens or lawns. They didn't really expect any trouble or fireworks—'The real scene of the action now is rural Kashmir,' I was told repeatedly—but they also added that 'you never know what will happen, even though the actual drama is already over in Srinagar'.

In south Kashmir, in the interiors of Pulwama and Anantnag, I had got a stronger sense of the prevalent mood. There were no major confrontations between the military and the militants, but there was a distinct sense of uncertainty and fear. The Médecins Sans Frontières counsellor Lynne Chobotar had told me weeks prior to the actual polling that though her team's work in the Pulwama district hospital took them there twice a week, they had stopped travelling on the Srinagar–Pulwama road during the election campaign. 'Call it a self-imposed curfew or whatever, but even in town we make it a point to be indoors by seven p.m.' She, however, dismissed any suggestion of political interference in their work, especially at this crucial juncture. 'None at all,' she said, 'I think politicians of this state don't even know of our existence ...'

I was travelling to these districts with four photojournalists. There were other journalists too, many familiar faces among them. The usual election jokes began early. When a cow appeared ahead of us, as if out of nowhere, one man quipped, 'How come Farooq Abdullah is here, staring at us in that overfed way?' Then two stray dogs wandered out from a nearby lane and someone said, 'Hope no security chap sees these poor doggies. I hear they have orders to shoot even newborn pups!' To which there was a loud addition: 'Naturally. They have been told that out of the 1025 booths 1000 are sensitive, and the rest are hypersensitive!' And so our party progressed merrily. You wouldn't have thought it was an election of great significance. But then, as my Kashmiri colleagues told me, they had begun to see humour in the strangest of situations. 'Survival tactics, if you may.'

We reached Pulwama early in the afternoon, where the security men and the few locals who were out in the streets all said that till then no votes had been cast. But in Kakapora we saw large numbers outside the polling booth. We were told that they were determined to ensure that the Congress candidate from their constituency won. They made no bones about this. When questioned about the militants' call to boycott the polls, they said that the call was for the ouster of the NC: 'We have been asked not to waste the vote; that means no voting for the NC. But we can vote for the Congress.' It was at this polling booth that I first encountered the strange phenomenon of being frisked by women draped in thick burqas. The veils covered their faces and figures so completely that it was impossible even to be sure if they weren't in fact men. I struck up a conversation just to be sure and was relieved when I heard replies in female voices. Why such elaborate burqas, I asked, and they confessed, 'We don't want anyone to see us. We don't want to be recognized.' But hadn't they been appointed by the government? 'Yes, but we just don't want our people to see us here, doing this job, frisking and all ...' All along the route thereafter, at almost every polling booth, this was a recurring sight—burqa-clad women, deputed to frisk women voters, sitting quietly at some distance from the security men.

Another near constant factor was the disgust of the young generation vis-à-vis the security forces, with accusatory fingers being pointed at the men from the Rashtriya Rifles. I have recounted earlier the incident of the boys in Shopian trembling at the sight of an RR man whom I had asked to pose with them for a photo. That particular officer seemed sensible and humane enough, but I was to see other well-built RR men intruding roughly into homes where terrified women screamed their lungs out at the sight of them. Young and old men had gathered outside some of the homes in one village and began pleading with us journalists that we should stay there so the jawans would be a bit restrained. Riazul Haque, a young teacher, was hysterical as he told us how he had nightmares about being detained. Two young girls cried out that the ailing Jamaat-i-Islami leader of Shopian town was being threatened that his 'fingers and hands will be chopped off'. We encountered similar sights in a majority of the villages we covered that day. There was some relief from the tension when we stopped to pluck some apples in a couple of places. Or when I met observers at the polling booths from my home state of Uttar Pradesh and we caught up on developments 'back home', and Farooq Abdullah jokes were replaced with those about Mayawati.

A week later, I was in Kupwara district, with my journalist

friends Fazili and Naqshbandi, this time for the re-polling at Lolab. By early morning, we had moved out of the municipal limits of Srinagar and were driving past Batamaloo, Qamarwari and the other outlying areas. In previous years, even about a decade ago, co-passengers would point out to me the special aspects of each town or village we passed—a famous dargah or ziarat of a Sufi or exotic crops cultivated in the area. This time, the names of the places were mentioned for different reasons—the number or nature of killings and custodial deaths; abductions and illegal detentions. The vehicle in which we were travelling was stopped somewhere along the way by a teenaged schoolboy, who told Fazili that his father Abdul Wani was to contest on a PDP ticket but just prior to filing his nomination papers he was arrested under POTA and then under the Public Safety Act. A rival group had engineered the arrest, he said. Our inquiries revealed that Abdul Wani was indeed very popular and would have definitely won if he hadn't been locked up.

At the polling station in Sogam, there were four booths side by side. They had a small, common entry gate, heavily guarded, with the result that there was only a slow trickle going in, although hundreds could be seen sitting on the sprawling grounds. The tension was palpable. Three crude explosive devices had gone off at the animal husbandry department nearby, minutes before we reached. The family of the slain NC minister Mushtaq Ahmad Lone, however, was there in full force. Qaiser, who had been fielded in place of his dead uncle, moved about weighed down by a bullet-proof jacket. Another uncle of his, Nazir Jowhar, who works as a food and civil supplies officer, wandered about, reciting Urdu verse. The subject of his verses had changed, he said to me, from romantic themes to the theme of indignity and humiliation: 'You can imagine how I must feel, being the son of the freedom fighter Haji Mohammad Muzaffar, when I'm asked to prove my very identity today, and that too to a jawan who isn't even from Kashmir and knows nothing about its history.'

That afternoon, near Kupwara town, Fazili and Naqshbandi went searching for an STD booth to file their stories while I stayed back, chatting with the bright-looking driver Shaukat Ahmad, a middle-aged Kashmiri from Srinagar. He told me he had worked earlier in New Delhi and also in Punjab. 'My sahib was also a Kashmiri, so the car had a JKD number plate and because of that cops in the capital would stop us at every possible place, throw suspicious looks at us.' Did he make many non-Muslim friends in the capital, I asked. 'No, I kept to myself, which wasn't difficult, though I'm a bachelor.' But he looked well beyond the marrying years, why hadn't he married—perhaps a Delhi woman? 'No, no,' he said hurriedly, 'definitely not a Hindu … See, it's okay for people like Omar Abdullah to marry outside their religion. I'm no one to criticize them, but they are different people, all too happy to put tikas on their foreheads and visit temples. But we are simple people.' Well, why didn't he marry someone from the community, then? 'But what's left here? What will I leave for my children? It's a terrible situation, so terrible that any cop on the road can throw you in jail or slit your throat or … No, you can't do anything about it, except crack jokes and have tea—my only two weaknesses!' And then he proceeded to have tea and tell me the choicest jokes about Ghulam Nabi Sogami, the politician of yore whose reputation for the inadvertently amusing is still legendary in parts of the Valley. Clearly, those were gentler times. The humour now is usually black.

On the way back we stopped at the main market of Kupwara, where I spotted a young man who looked like someone from my state, Uttar Pradesh. Young Ziauddin, barely out of his teens, told me that he hailed from Sitapur but every year around this time he came to sell blankets and shawls in the villages here. I was surprised and wanted to know if he never felt fearful, given that this particular belt saw more than its share of militant strikes and counter-insurgency operations. His response, more cynical than even that of most Kashmiris I had spoken to, startled me. '*Bhookh se ya goli se, marna toh hai* [Hunger or the bullet, one will die either way],' he said lightly. '*Goli se ho toh jaldi chhutti pa lein* [At least the bullet will be quicker].'

*

Having travelled through several towns and villages during the 2002 polls, I would say that the elections were reasonably fair, but clearly not without fear, particularly in rural Kashmir. The atmosphere was one of terror of the army and mistrust of the ruling government in particular and politicians in general. The result was a defiance of the whole election exercise by many through a boycott, while most of those who did vote seemed to have done so without any great enthusiasm and just to buy peace. Supervised by the Election Commission, the local civil administration and the police and security forces had put in place an enormous and mostly effective infrastructure of polling booths and polling staff. But there was clear evidence that electoral rolls had not been revised in some places and there were not enough identity cards in others. There were also complaints that the security forces had made announcements about the polls from mosques, herded people to the polling stations in some areas and forced minors and non-voters to cast their votes. There were no women police in many booths and outside several others there were armed renegades in full view.

Despite the fear, though, this time people spoke out, perhaps because there were a large number of journalists, foreign observers and human rights groups touring the Valley. People talked openly about human rights abuses, corruption, lack of development, and about azadi. Even those who had decided to boycott the elections took the opportunity to make themselves heard. After the azadi and zulm (tyranny) had been talked about and got out of the way, the complaints that followed sounded much like what one would hear at election time in any other part of India. As the Institute of Social Sciences observed in its report on the elections:

> Many times the team members felt they were talking to people in the villages of Madhya Pradesh or Bihar. Poor quality of roads, growing unemployment, distance from the government machinery and unsympathetic government employees and politicians were issues of the people there too. What was surprising was that while in the rest of the country people would blame panchayats for not doing anything, in the Valley there was no mention of panchayats and urban local bodies anywhere. People were blaming the chief minister, the state government and the Central government for all the problems they were facing.

The militants hadn't been entirely quiet either. Threats from the militants were relayed through posters and there was violence, including grenade attacks, at polling stations. But few people talked openly about this. On the subject of coercion by the security forces there was no such reserve, though there were also those who denied that they had been forced to vote by the army. It could also be said that some people who wanted to vote were using the excuse of coercion by the security forces to protect themselves from the wrath of the militants. Generally, though, it was a good sign, relatively speaking, that on polling days both the queues of those who had decided to vote and groups of those who had decided not to were equally visible. It was, overall, an election in which people were free to either exercise their right to vote or not.

In its exhaustive report, the Institute of Social Sciences had listed the three things that it felt the Indian government wanted to prove through these elections:

Kashmir is not under the political influence of militant groups, who want separation from India; the people believe in democracy and democratic methods of change in government; and the present system adequately serves them as it allows them the freedom to exercise their choice.

Partially—and only partially—India appeared to have succeeded in doing so. But I was concerned by the self-congratulatory euphoria that followed. It was marked by the same old refusal to confront the real problem.

The Elections and After

On the morning of 10 October 2002, as the very first election results started coming in, I spotted a rather nervous-looking director of information, S. Narinder Singh, pacing the lawns of the Tourist Reception Centre. He was soon joined by two other civil servants, who had probably got an inkling by now of the impending rout of the National Conference. They approached Narinder Singh, and I overheard them say, 'Sir, you're already walking in reverse gear!' (As it turned out, in the administrative reshuffle that followed, Narinder Singh was shunted out of his coveted post to look after the municipality of Jammu city.) That was the first confirmation for me of what many of us journalists had suspected for some time—that the NC did not stand a chance of coming back to power, provided of course the elections were reasonably free and fair. The incumbent chief minister, Farooq Abdullah, himself was away in South Africa, but several of the bureaucrats considered part of his inner circle—I.S. Malhi, B.R. Singh and Ashok Jaitly, besides Narinder Singh—were around, and pretty soon they were becoming the subject of subtle jokes in Kashmiri.

Farooq Abdullah had put his son Omar in charge of the NC before the polls. It is difficult to say if he did this because he realized how much of a liability he personally had become for his party. Or if he understood just how low the NC's image had plummeted. His alliance with the Congress in the mid-1980s, the absence of any real engagement with ordinary Kashmiris, and of course his decision to join the BJP-led government at the Centre had all served to turn Kashmiris away from him and his party. Added to all these were allegations of massive corruption.

Charges of corruption have continued to appear in newspaper reports even months after the 2002 elections. In a report in the *Indian Express* of 24 August 2003, Tariq Mir ripped apart Omar Abdullah's claims about how he had spent the two crore rupees given to him as a member of Parliament under the Local Area Development Scheme. Roughly three months later (9 December 2003), Saleem Pandit wrote in the *Times of India*, in a report entitled 'Anti-terror Fund Lines VIP Nests', that in the fifteen years of insurgency in the state, while a 'a tidal wave of Union money' was pouring in, no satisfactory system had been put in place to keep track of all the cash flowing in from Delhi. The obvious result of this was that 'money from the Security Related Expenditure head has been, and continues to be used, for carpets, geysers, TV sets and the like for the State's VIPs'. The report went on to quote the deputy accountant general, Sanjay Goyal, as saying that the 'mis-utilized' funds amounted to approximately eight crore a year in the period between 1996 and 2001 (when the NC was in power). Another daily detailed the PTI news item on the comptroller and auditor general's report which listed financial irregularities that 'deprived the state of rupees 12.51 crore Central assistance' between 1997 and 2002.

But corruption and insensitivity apart—the people expected nothing better, perhaps—the issue that seemed to have done the greatest damage to the NC's chances immediately before the elections was that of the Gujarat riots.

Even unlettered Kashmiris I met in Srinagar prior to the actual polling had seen images of the carnage on TV and in newspapers and this had had a definite effect on their psyche. As several Kashmiris told me, even the demolition of the Babri Masjid hadn't caused such a reaction in the state. An elderly bakery owner whom I had befriended over the years naively asked how I had been spared by Modi, before adding gravely, 'You got away because you live in New Delhi, I think, and Gujarat is far from there, isn't it?' The ghosts of Gujarat were all over the city. 'Farooq Abdullah's politician friends are killing my community in Gujarat and he's quiet ... Now if the polls and results are fair, you watch how he'll be thrown out,' said a houseboat owner. He remembered spotting a group of Gujarati tourists walking down the Boulevard while the rioting and connected atrocities were at their peak in Ahmedabad. 'My blood boiled,' he told me. 'I should have cut them to pieces. But I just couldn't bring myself to think along those lines.' Even a moderate, soft-spoken politician like Saifuddin Soz said that he had felt disgusted at the turn of events: 'It's the same Farooq Abdullah who had won the last elections by criticizing the right-wing forces and now he is with them, even after the blatant massacre of Muslims in Gujarat.' It was only in July 2003, over a year after the riots, that Omar Abdullah pulled out of the NDA government, citing as reasons the Central government's insensitivity towards Kashmir and its conduct during the Gujarat riots. By then the move could only be seen as pure farce.

It is likely that even if Gujarat hadn't happened, the NC would have been voted out. But when Farooq and Omar chose political opportunism—those more generously inclined towards them might call it pragmatism—over principles and the sentiments of fellow Kashmiris, a large majority of whom are Muslims, they sealed their fate completely. Which, given the past record of their government, was perhaps a good thing for Kashmir.

On the day the election results were declared, I was warned by several friends that I shouldn't move about in Srinagar unless absolutely necessary; they felt the National Conference defeat would anger the party's sympathizers and there might be trouble. I decided to risk it nevertheless. As I walked towards Raj Bagh for an interview with Shabir Shah, the residents of Srinagar I saw on the roads seemed in an upbeat mood. There were several smiling faces—a rare sight in Srinagar. Colleagues were to recount, later in the day, that even the cops at the counting centre in Centaur Hotel were unable to mask their smiles as results began trickling out. On my way back from Raj Bagh in an auto, I realized I was short of change, and when I said this to the driver very apologetically, he waved a hand and said, 'I'm so happy we've managed to defeat the NC today that even if you don't pay me a single rupee it would be okay!' Similar sentiments were expressed at the STD booth I frequented, where people couldn't conceal their excitement, though most of them added rather sheepishly, 'No, no, we didn't vote, but these results are what we wanted—we just wanted this NC government out.' The STD booth was close to the main bus stop, where there was a large group of Kashmiri Muslims from different parts of the Valley. All of them looked excited and confidently defiant. It was a special mood for Srinagar. I saw a young Sikh boy a little distance from the bus stop, giggling happily, and I asked him the reason. 'If they're happy,' he said, pointing to the group, 'so am I!'

The cyber café where I went to file my story was empty

for a change. Groups of boys and young men were huddled outside, busy exchanging notes on the results. A few of them asked me whether Farooq was packing his bags for the UK to shift into the hotel he was rumoured to have set up in Central London with his friend Yusuf Khan, chairman of the Jammu and Kashmir Bank. Gupkar Road, where the Abdullahs live, was empty, but for the security men. It was gloom time here. By the following morning security had slackened. A golf enthusiast reported driving down the road to reach the Royal Springs Golf Course—till just a day earlier, no private vehicle without a pass for proof of residence would have been allowed on this road.

The scenes of victory, of course, were being played out at the Nowgam residence of the Muftis. Since the true significance of these elections was in the context of the Kashmir Valley, to understand the magnitude of the NC's defeat, we must limit ourselves to results in the Valley (rather than the entire state of Jammu and Kashmir). Mufti Mohammad Sayeed and his daughter Mehbooba Mufti had led the PDP to victory in sixteen seats in the Valley. The NC's tally of forty in the 1996 elections had come down to eighteen. The remaining seats were won by the Congress (5), and others (7), comprising independents, the Panthers Party and CPI (M). When I phoned to ask for the PDP's comments, it was Mufti Mohammad Sayeed who took the call and said that since Mehbooba would be returning late from Anantnag, I could come over the next morning. I reached the sprawling bungalow in the morning to find the entire complex flooded with people. The security wasn't too tight and ordinary Kashmiris and PDP MLAs and their supporters milled around together. Cups of kehwa were freely available. Men threw garlands at the freshly elected candidates. But the focus was clearly on Mehbooba, dressed in a black churidar kurta. In keeping with the traditions of the region, men did not embrace her but many went up to her and congratulated her, clutching her hand with great affection. Women hugged her. It was clear that the Mufti's daughter was the real hero; she had won the elections for her party with her tireless and sensitive campaigning and her work among the people of the Valley. She spoke to each person, many a time addressing them by their first names. Not having met her before, I tried my luck for an interview. She agreed readily, without fuss, and asked a party worker to take me up to the living room on the first floor—'that's the only place where we can talk without much disturbance'—and added that she would follow.

As I waited, a party worker, Gulzar Hussain, told me that he had decided to join the PDP only after his interaction with Mehbooba. 'I haven't seen such a politician in today's times ... if you call up even at midnight that STF men have barged into your home, she will be there to fight on your behalf, ask them the reasons for the intrusion.'

Mehbooba arrived shortly afterwards, looking every bit a warm but determined woman. As a single parent to two teenaged daughters, she said, she wouldn't ordinarily have thought of politics. She had taken the plunge out of family compulsions. 'Somebody had to represent our home constituency of Bijbehara and I did so without knowing a thing about politics ... ignorance really is bliss, I suppose ... Usually, the sons of the family take to politics but my only brother Tasadduq had moved to Hollywood, where he works as a director.' She was forthright to the extent of saying that elections were definitely not the final solution to the Kashmir crisis. 'Our priority will be to see to it that our people are not humiliated. I've seen how young boys are punished, made to sit by the side of the road if they are not carrying their I-cards

... and I'm aware of the humiliation they face when they are in the capital. New Delhi here stands for crackdowns, interrogations.' I was to meet Mehbooba again some months later, and once again came away with the impression that she holds out definite promise as an effective leader of her people. She seems to be an elder sister to thousands in the rural belt around Srinagar city, where people invariably recount instances when she helped them in times of crises.

There were victory celebrations in one suite of the Tourist Reception Centre as well, where Bhim Singh, the chief of the Panthers Party, was staying. Bhim Singh and the documentary film-maker Nasreen Hameed were surrounded by victorious candidates of the Panthers Party and some straying Congressmen. There was considerable confusion about the alliance that would be worked out—as they put it, the 'mathematics is unclear'—since no single party had won a majority. All of them, however, seemed to be rejoicing in the defeat of the NC. Bhim Singh did come up with a lament of sorts. Referring to the true victors in the elections, he said, '*Haathi woh le gaye, aur dum mere saath chhodi hai* [They've taken the elephant and left only the tail for me].' But he recovered quickly and told me how news of his personal victory was celebrated in jails throughout the state. 'After all,' he said, 'I'm fighting for fifty of those imprisoned ... I've also lived in jails for over eight and a half years—Shabir and I were imprisoned around the same time. Even Mufti and I have shared the same jail cell in Jammu.' By now it was afternoon and it was clear how badly the ruling NC had lost, but Bhim Singh wanted me to know that the outgoing government had tried every dirty trick in the book. 'Even for these elections the establishment played a mischievous role. Just see the flaws in the election list. They used the voters list of 1988, without omitting about one lakh names of those who died in this period, including the name of Farooq Abdullah's dead mother, Akbar Jahaan—and the age that's been given next to her name is seventy years, though Farooq Abdullah himself must be only a couple of years short of seventy! There have been more blunders on this list ... Karan Singh's wife's name is not given...' He was soon joined by a local Congressman, Abdul Ghani Khan, who had won from the Idgah constituency. He was equipped with a bunch of photographs to prove his charge that there was bogus voting too. 'Three vans were given to the STF to bring in mobile voters ... I saw the whole exercise ... you also see it in these photographs.'

I could also sense that Bhim Singh hadn't given up hope of occupying the chief minister's seat, improbable though this seemed. Apropos of nothing, he said to me, 'This is such a secular state, so it is apt that a non-Muslim, a Dogra from Jammu, should be chief minister ... No, no, don't misunderstand me, I'm not saying make me the chief minister. But why not? Inmates in jails will be so happy with the news!' In the time it eventually took the PDP and the Congress to finally agree on an alliance, Bhim Singh, like some others, must have fancied his chances more than once.

The main action, as far as the formation of the next government was concerned, was taking place at Hotel Broadway. It was here that Congressmen had gathered to prove their majority. They had won twenty seats, though fifteen of these were in Jammu and only five in the Valley, and were hoping to pull together the independents and even some PDP MLAs to muster a majority. The lounge, the poolside and the rooms were all occupied by party workers and it seemed an open house. If you even hinted that you wanted an interview with any of the Congressmen, right from Ghulam Nabi Azad, who led the Congress in the state for the elections, to Saifuddin Soz or the Jammu Congressman Mangat Ram Sharma, you could be sure of a prompt invitation to Broadway, to be fussed upon in one of the rooms where the congregation could be seen sitting, huddled anxiously like overgrown schoolboys, waiting to hear from Madam in Delhi.

Differences between Congress workers from Jammu and those from Srinagar were more than apparent and that was probably one of the reasons why a Congress chief minister could not be installed. Saifuddin Soz, though, seemed more than hopeful right till the end. Around the time it became clear that any alliance to form a government would have to include the Congress, I met Soz and he hinted that he was in the race. This despite the fact that he had joined the Congress just a few weeks prior to the elections, having parted ways with Farooq Abdullah in disgust because for three years he had been telling 'him [Farooq] and other NC members to mend their ways but they didn't pay any heed'.

A PDP chief minister was nowhere in the scheme of things for weeks after the results. The state Congress, with the larger number of seats, was determined to have its own person heading the government. But the PDP was clear that it wouldn't join any coalition unless Mufti Mohammad Sayeed was made the chief minister. On 19 October the then Jammu and Kashmir governor Girish Chandra Saxena held a press conference at Raj Bhavan and it seemed that the only option now was governor's rule, since there seemed no possibility of a majority emerging. 'I can't comment on the extent of governor's rule. I would like to keep it as short as possible,' Saxena said, and also made it clear that he would not be appointing any advisors 'for the time being'. Saxena, a former RAW chief, was an experienced man (he had played an important role during the formation of Bangladesh, and was even rumoured to have lived posing as a maulvi in a Dhaka mosque at the time) and naturally he was extremely careful with each reply he gave to the queries put to him. Yet, the general perception after the press conference was that governor's rule was now inevitable.

Eventually, though, the PDP and the Congress did come together to form a government. It is said that I.K. Gujral was instrumental in this. He impressed upon the Congress that after all the effort that had gone into holding the elections, the situation could not be allowed to get out of control and the Mufti—one-time colleague and a close friend—was the best choice and shouldn't be out of bounds for the Congress. Mufti Mohammad Sayeed was sworn in as chief minister on 2 November 2002. Only the day before, in a coincidence that some people hopeful of a new turn in Kashmir's politics must have seen as a welcome omen, a Srinagar court ordered the release on bail of five militants, among them a senior JKLF leader who was the main accused in the kidnapping of the Mufti's daughter Rubaiya in 1989.

*

I began writing this book several weeks after the 2002 elections, and work on it continued for over a year. Much has happened in the Valley since, but the picture is certainly not clear. Perhaps as unclear as the recently announced Indo–Pak talks and what they will mean for the people of Kashmir.

There have been some positive signs, but look at them closely and many seem only superficially positive. One such would be the series of visits by major political leaders to the Valley. Prime Minister Vajpayee was there for a two-day visit in April 2003 and then again for the chief ministers' conference in August, attended also by the deputy prime minister, L.K. Advani; and Sonia Gandhi flew in late May for the Congress chief ministers' conclave. The President, Dr Abdul Kalam, also visited the Valley in June 2003. All this has made little difference to the lives of the people in the Valley. What does hold promise is the upswing in the numbers of the tourists, beginning in the summer of 2003, right up to December. In December the figure touched 200 tourists a day with hundred per cent bookings in Gulmarg. The following month, the Fourth National Winter Games were held in Gulmarg. This, more than the VVIP visits, helped give the impression that the Valley was a reasonably safe place for a tourist.

Mufti Mohammad Sayeed started off as the chief minister of Jammu and Kashmir with a 'clean image', in contrast to that of his predecessor, and he has been keen to build on this image. Within months of his swearing in, thirteen government departments, among them the departments of excise, sales tax, forest, rural development, transport, and food and supplies, were brought under the State Vigilance Organization. The PDP-led government also promulgated an ordinance to take over eighty-nine shrines of the Valley (including Hazratbal and Charar-i-Sharief), thus dismantling the Muslim Auqaf Trust headed by the former chief minister—the explanation was that this move was necessary to prevent the swindling of funds collected as donations. Farooq Abdullah's favourite Royal Springs Golf Course, which had become almost his private playground, was also put to good use, for what was referred to as 'golf diplomacy'—envoys of several countries were invited to play there for the Ambassador's Golf Cup.

Other initiatives included a 179-crore-rupee project to restore Wular Lake, a plan to set up a seventeen-crore-rupee national fruit market in Sopore, and the launch, eight years after cellphones first came to India, of mobile phone services in Srinagar. For the first time in fifteen years, the National Literacy Mission and the state administration came together to launch a scheme for adult education in the state. The new chief minister also led a seven-member team to London to attend the World Tourism Mart and promote his state as an ideal tourist destination. Finally, it seemed, Kashmir had a government concerned more with development than with crowding the streets of Srinagar with armed men and tanks.

But disillusionment appears to have set in already. After a year and a half of the PDP-led coalition's rule, there isn't as much enthusiasm for the new dispensation as there was in the first few euphoric months, and quite a few people I spoke to were dismissive of the government's grand announcements.

One of the biggest grievances against the Mufti government is its inability to tackle the problem of unemployment. Extravagant promises were made: more ITIs to be opened, one lakh new jobs to be created. But the employment situation remains grim. There are over 1.7 lakh educated youth registered with the state employment department. This, together with the continuing searches, random interrogations and the attendant humiliation, and the general stress of living in a strife-ravaged society, is still driving the young to anti-depressant drugs. Dr Hameeda Jan, chairperson of the de-addiction and rehabilitation centre in downtown Srinagar, confirms that addiction is on the rise in the Valley and that it is 'directly related to continuing violence and rising unemployment'. Responding to questions about employment by a journalist of the *Times of India*, Mufti Sayeed put the blame on the country's private sector. He was disappointed with the corporate sector, he said. There were no serious proposals for investment. 'Everyone keeps talking about how Kashmir is at the core of India's nationhood. But if it is so important, why then are the industrialists not coming forward?' It was a frustration that a chief minister keen to be seen in control should perhaps not have made so public. Especially when there is increasing criticism that instead of concentrating on real development, the Mufti is playing to the Centre. Kashmiri friends have told me that they are no longer impressed when there are announcements to the effect that the border posts of Suchetgarh and Uri in the Kashmir Valley could be opened. How long, asked a friend, will the people of Kashmir be swayed by slogans of a bus service between Srinagar and Muzaffarabad? They also point out that custodial and encounter deaths are continuing, even though they concede that the chief minister is, after all, heading a coalition government and security-related issues are usually handled by the army and the paramilitary over which he has no direct control.

Perhaps the worst criticism has to do with the Mufti's nod to an amendment in the Transfer of Property Act. The amendment provides for the mortgage of immovable property in favour of financial institutions and banks so that loans can be raised for development projects in Jammu and Kashmir. This move is being seen as undermining Article 370 which bars non-Kashmiris from acquiring rights over immovable property in the state. Even the usually circumspect Mirwaiz Umar Farooq accused the chief minister of 'conspiring to change the state's demography'. It is clearly a touchy issue and it isn't going to win the chief minister too many supporters in the Valley, even if he explains that such radical measures are necessary to get funds into the Valley, without which development projects—like the Kishen Ganga Hydroelectric Project to generate 330 MW of power—can never take off.

Meanwhile, ugly incidents continue. Twenty-four innocent Kashmiri Pandits were massacred in Nadimarg in south Kashmir. Residents of the region were stunned and baffled: how could the killers have moved about so freely, they wondered. Some even saw it as an effort to undermine the Mufti and his policy of reaching out and talking to the disaffected lot who may have taken to violence. Perhaps there is some truth in this since there were reports soon after that there would be a halt in the release of prisoners. The incident also set back the PDP's efforts to bring back Pandit families and help them resettle in Khirbhawani, Mattan, Sheikhpora and Anantnag. Which Pandit family will risk returning now, and who will take the responsibility for their safety? More disturbing is the fact that as yet there has been no inquiry by a totally independent agency into the gruesome massacre.

The PDP's main promise to the electorate had been that it would bring the much-needed 'healing touch' to the Valley. Some prisoners were indeed released, but this alone doesn't add up to much. The number of suspected custodial deaths has not come down, and most of the victims are, as before, young Muslim men from the Valley. On 18 July 2003, the *Indian Express* reported that there had been three custodial deaths in three days. The most shameful incident took place in September 2003. Twenty-two-year-old Tahir Hassan Maqdoomi was picked up by the army from Tujjar Sharief (Sopore) shortly after his marriage ceremony had been completed. Three days later the family were told that he had died in a mine blast. The army claimed that he was their 'guide' and the explosion that killed him had taken place at a militant camp. The young bride and his parents were handed over parts of his body.

In November, a sleepy village in Bandipora erupted in protest after the army came raiding at dawn, looking for Haneefa's daughter. The family was deep in sleep, but the army men at the doorstep wouldn't wait, they wanted to take the twenty-year-old away for questioning immediately. They accused her of being a conduit for militants. Before knocking on Haneefa's door, the jawans had raided the neighbouring house of Abdul Rashid Jan, a retired policeman, and picked up his fifteen-year-old son Javed Ahmad. 'They came disguised as militants ... they forcibly took my son and when we raised an alarm, they ran towards an army camp,' Abdul Rashid was quoted as saying in the *Indian Express*. 'We tried to follow but stopped after they fired in the air ... Around noon the army admitted that he was with them ... If the army had to arrest him, why did they have to come disguised as militants?'

There have been other tragedies. In June, a thirteen-year-old and his father Abdul Qayoom Peer, an imam, were shot dead by the army in village Vayil in north Kashmir in a case of mistaken identity. There are also cases where confusion reigns over who exactly is responsible for the killings or abductions and torture, the army or the militants—as in the case of two sisters, a police constable's teenaged daughters, who alleged that they were shot at by Rashtriya Rifles personnel, but the army insisted that it was a clear case of militants trying to settle scores. In the absence of any thorough investigations, such confusion is inevitable. On 23 January 2004, when I interviewed the Hurriyat chairman Maulana Abbas Ansari, he said, 'Even now, every day we are losing five to ten of our people ... even in this month of January we have lost almost hundred people.' I asked him who was killing whom, and he shot back, 'Don't ask me who is killing whom. There are bunkers on the roads and even if a stone is thrown at them there is indiscriminate firing and several innocent civilians die.'

Through 2003, there were blasts, landmine explosions and grenade attacks by militants. Several people were killed, many others were left seriously injured and maimed with splinters and shrapnel in their flesh. An article in the *Hindustan Times* (24 July 2003) reported that 'hundreds of Kashmiris live and die with splinters in their flesh—splinters which tear away at lightning speed after a grenade explodes ... some die, several are maimed while others live with shrapnel embedded in their bodies ... ragged stitch lines are visible on every fourth patient admitted at the SMHS hospital'. There were blasts and explosions in Srinagar's main vegetable market and the crowded Lal Chowk shopping area, in the Amira Kadal locality which lies in the heart of the city, and one just outside the chief minister's residence. The interiors weren't safe either: in Khulbagh, Tral, a blast killed six people and several others suffered splinter injuries. Terror attacks aimed at the armed forces continued. In each case army men and civilians lost their lives.

Young men and boys still 'disappear'. Despite the PDP's promise to track down the Valley's missing, the old cases remain unsolved, while new ones are added almost every day. The National Human Rights Commission was constrained to voice its concern over the 'unsatisfactory and vague reply of the J&K government regarding the enforced or involuntary disappearance of people in the state'.

The most shocking case was reported as late as February 2004. On the ninth of that month newspapers carried a report that five civilian porters in Bandipora had been killed, allegedly by the army. The *Indian Express* carried the eyewitness account of a survivor, Mohammad Yusuf Bani. Apparently, Bani and his brother were taken from their homes by men in army uniforms and asked to guide them through the forest close to their village. When they entered the forest, however, there were already armed jawans in a trench there. As daylight broke, the jawans began firing mortars at a bunker where they claimed some militants were holed up. 'An officer told us to go inside the bunker and see who was there,' Bani reported. When they protested, they were told that if they didn't, for fear of the militants' bullets, they would have to take the army's bullets. 'When we got there,' said Bani, 'the army fired and hit my brother. I crawled to the bunker, but there was no firing from there, it was empty.' His brother bled to death. Shortly afterwards the jawans brought four more civilians. These men were asked to put on army uniforms and then asked to go up to the bunker and clear the debris. Then the jawans fired, killing all four. An inquiry was ordered after the report was published, but what can it mean to the families? And as the villagers point out, if Bani had not survived to tell the gory tale, there would have been no inquiry. They would probably have been told that the men were gunned down by unknown militants.

But it must be said here that in Mufti Sayeed's Kashmir, the authorities have begun to look seriously at reported cases of killings, disappearances or torture, and the government at least announces some relief and orders a judicial or magisterial inquiry. In June 2003, the state government dismissed a deputy superintendent of police, Abdul Rashid Khan, allegedly responsible for the deaths of three persons in custody in 1999. In September, taking suo motu action on media reports regarding a firing incident by the Indo Tibetan Border Police (ITBP) in Anantnag on 30 August 2002 that left four civilians seriously injured, the J&K State Human Rights Commission issued notices to top police officers, directing them to register a FIR against the ITBP men. In October, upholding the indictment of the police by the State Human Rights Commission in the disappearance of a government employee in 1997, the J&K High Court ordered the state government to register a criminal case against the erring officials and complete the investigation within four months. The following month, holding the army responsible for the custodial death of a young man, the State Human Rights Commission directed the J&K government to pay two lakh rupees to the victim's family. With the government taking the lead, the security forces too are keen to be seen as responsible and sensitive. The General Officer Commanding (GOC) 15 Corps, Lieutenant General V.G. Patankar, issued a categorical statement in May 2003 (reported in the *Tribune*, 28 May 2003): 'We have issued clear instructions to troops engaged in counter-insurgency that the common man should not be harassed ... no indiscipline will be tolerated by us.'

Outside the Valley, Kashmiri youth found no respite. Hoping for a safe place away from the might of the security forces and the threat of the militants, many of them walked into nightmares in Delhi and other cities and small towns in India. I have detailed in a previous chapter the case of Kashmiri students in Uttar Pradesh who were picked up and wrongfully detained on mere suspicion that they were dreaded militants. In October 2003, in Thane, Maharashtra, four Kashmiri youth were paraded as Hizbul Mujahideen militants. They were charged with possession of arms, accused of plotting to kill prominent Maharashtra politicians and were later handed over to the J&K police, but the investigations that followed came up with little to prove that the four, who worked as security guards, were militants. The Thane police, however, returned with more 'secret' evidence and the four were sentenced to life imprisonment. In Punjab, a group of Kashmiri men from Shopian were intercepted near Amritsar by the police, who were sure they had found 'dangerous terrorists'. When IGP Rajendra was contacted in Srinagar, he was incredulous. The men were Mirzayi Muslims on their way back from a wedding in Qadian, Punjab. 'We were surprised when we heard about these arrests,' said Rajendra, 'there's no one from this community who has ever been involved in militancy.'

And then there was the well-publicized case, in April 2003, of a seventeen-year-old Kashmiri rickshaw-puller, Basheer Ahmed Dar, who was allegedly picked up by the Delhi Police from the Old Delhi railway station a few days after the 13 December 2001 attack on Parliament. According to him, he was tortured at various police stations in the capital for thirteen months before eventually being returned to Srinagar. When journalists met him in the SMHS hospital, there was clear evidence of torture. There were other marks—tattoos of Hindu gods—etched on his body by a policeman in Lajpat Nagar: 'This is Bajrangbali,' he said, lifting his shirt sleeve, 'and this is Om with a snake...'

Mehbooba Mufti took up the matter of Kashmiri students being harassed in UP and elsewhere with the Centre, but such interventions can be no substitute for a sensitive and clearly stated policy. In the absence of such a policy, the psyche of young Kashmiri Muslims will continue to be affected, which does not augur well for the future. Why should the security personnel who continue to make these reckless arrests not be held accountable? Why should it take over twelve years for a politician to take up the case of Parveena Ahangar's son who was picked up for interrogation by the BSF and is yet to be traced? There are other serious issues that need to be addressed. The chairman of the National Human Rights Commission, Justice A.S. Anand, responding to my query about an allegation that some female students had been molested by army personnel in Shopian, south Kashmir, made an astonishing revelation. 'We are pursing the case and have written to the army to furnish the report,' he said. 'But even a body like the NHRC cannot investigate directly ... Though the Protection of Human Rights Act of 1993 confers the power upon the Commission to inquire into and investigate allegations of violation of human rights by the civil authorities, according to Section 19 of the Act that pertains to complaints of violations by members of the armed forces, the Commission can only seek a report from the Central government and can make recommendations on the basis of that report. It cannot investigate the complaints directly.'

*

Those genuinely interested in an end to the turmoil in the Valley had high hopes of the government that took over after a reasonably fair election—after decades—in Jammu and Kashmir. Many of them still do, though no one seriously believes that the Mufti's government has the power to effect any lasting change—there are too many big players with a stake in the mess that is Kashmir; India and Pakistan are only two most directly involved and conspicuous parties. What the hopeful lot see, though, is a window of opportunity, and keep their fingers crossed.

In an interview dated 26 September 2003 with Mahesh Daga of the *Times of India*, the new chief minister conceded that politically the state had suffered because of 'the lack of progress' in relations between India and Pakistan, and that this continues to be a problem. But he maintained that while in the past human rights violations were the order of the day, 'you have to appreciate that there has been a change in the attitude and role of the security forces'. During an earlier interview he gave me, I asked him about his equation with New Delhi, especially in the context of his policies in Kashmir being labelled 'soft' by hardliners in the coalition at the Centre. 'What do you mean by soft policies?' the Mufti shot back. 'I'm trying to talk to the people, enter into a dialogue. The gun has not served any purpose. We have to end this alienation—today the Kashmiri wants to live with dignity and in peace.' Was he saying that the Kashmiri had not known dignity and peace in the past? To that the chief minister said, 'In response to this let me quote Prime Minister Atal Behari Vajpayee, who has said, "We may have committed some mistakes in Kashmir ... we will talk to the elected representatives and other sections of government."'

In keeping with the popular mood in the Valley, the idea of American intervention of any kind did not seem to enthuse the Mufti. In the same interview, he had stressed, 'We have to solve our problem ourselves and not go to the USA with a begging bowl. *America kya karega*? [What can America do for us?]' This was even before the US Deputy Secretary of State Richard Armitage had declared Kashmir as 'the most dangerous place in the world' after Israel and Palestine, and the US government had sent Mehbooba Mufti an invitation for a State Department-sponsored seminar on Kashmir which she tactfully turned down.

But to Kashmiris pleased with the categorical stand taken against foreign meddling by their chief minister, it must have come as a bit of a shock that an entirely different kind of foreign presence, and a completely baffling one, seemed to have sneaked into the Valley without any protest from the state government. In September 2003, it was reported that the British chief of defence staff was in Srinagar, accompanied by British military officials, to hold meetings with the senior army officers of the 15 Corps. Soon afterwards came the news that a British police station would be set up in Srinagar. Apparently, the West Midlands police were planning to open a station in Srinagar to track down criminals who fled to Kashmir after committing crimes in the UK! Up to twenty-eight officers, half of them British, will be based in Srinagar, the first overseas station for a British police force. One detective from West Midlands had already been to Jammu and Kashmir earlier that year. It was a bizarre case. Some puzzled Kashmiris I spoke to asked openly, 'Is this the return of the dreaded *gori fauj* [white army] or what?' Given that so much about their own affairs appears murky to people in the Valley, such shady developments are the last thing any administration should encourage. Unfortunately, there was no reaction or clarification from the government; in fact, the only party in Kashmir that reacted strongly to the news was the Panthers Party.

For the moment, though, the new state government appears not to have lost its way and it is possible to hope that at least some of the mistakes of the past can be undone and some of the wounds healed. A complete solution is still too much to wish for, because though India and Pakistan have made noises about peace, about discussing Kashmir and fighting terrorism of every kind, the future of Kashmir remains out of the hands of its people. It is tempting to think that all the suffering that the people of Jammu and Kashmir have experienced can be wiped away by some magical solution designed primarily to help both India and Pakistan save face. A National Conference MLA, who had won in the last elections with a comfortable majority, said to me recently, 'Now it all depends on what India and Pakistan want ... it will take them just twenty-four hours to sort out the basic issues. Otherwise the situation cannot really change. There will be slight changes but nothing drastic.' Members of the present government in the state say pretty much the same thing.

Outside the government there has been a major change. Maulana Abbas Ansari, a moderate, took over as chief of the

All Party Hurriyat Conference (APHC), the conglomerate of separatist groups, in July 2003. But soon after assuming office he made it clear that he would not talk to anyone other than the PM: 'If he [the PM] sends his secretary, I will send mine.' Later, for the first round of the much publicized Hurriyat–Centre meet on 22 January 2004, it was Deputy Prime Minister L.K. Advani that the Hurriyat Conference delegation led by Maulana Abbas Ansari met in New Delhi. The Hurriyat leaders did call on Prime Minister Vajpayee too, but that was just a 'courtesy call'. When I asked Abbas Ansari whether in the last six months he had softened his stand, given his earlier proclamations about having nothing to do with N.N. Vohra, the interlocutor appointed by the Centre, he said, 'My views about Vohra remain the same. He is just a retired bureaucrat and I strongly feel that any *mulaqaat* between the government and us has to be on a certain level. Though Vohra was present at our meeting with Advani sahib, he was silent throughout. Advani sahib did all the talking ... And why should we be criticized for this dialogue with the Centre? Didn't Mahatma Gandhi and Nelson Mandela hold talks with the British?' (Abbas Ansari was indirectly referring to the criticism he had been facing from the breakaway faction of the Hurriyat led by Syed Ali Shah Geelani, and also by leaders of the two factions who did not attend these talks—Yasin Malik of the JKLF and Shabir Shah of the Democratic Freedom Party.)

Abbas Ansari was quite categorical that till the average Kashmiri is asked what he wants and is heard, there can be no solution. The Centre's call for a ceasefire didn't seem to mean too much to him. The 'Mujahideen' had not responded to it, he said, and with good reason. 'They are not sure of the Government of India's sincerity ... How would they believe that GOI is sincere when my passport has been taken away and I haven't even been allowed to go to Mecca for Haj or to any ziarat [across the border] ... It is really a sad situation that we can't meet people from the other side [of Kashmir] even though only a distance of about fifteen minutes separates us.'

So, clearly, the much-touted talks will do nothing more than the usual—the old story of one step forward and two back. A truly lasting solution to the Kashmir issue might in fact require something far more radical than anyone dares to think of. It is suggested in an old file that Professor Shahid Siddiqi dug out for me. The file contains the correspondence between his father-in-law Major General E. Habibullah and Nehru. Habibullah suggests a federation of India, Pakistan and Kashmir 'as a possible solution to the crisis'. In his letter dated 20 February 1963, Nehru replies:

> I agree with much that you say about India and Pakistan. But it is not at all clear to me what I can do in the matter at present. As you know, I gave a hint the other day that there might be a loose federation between India and Pakistan. The result was furore in Pakistan, or, at any rate, in the governing circles and the press there. If I repeat this, the reaction will be worse. We have to deal with those in authority in Pakistan and they will not agree to any such proposal and will interpret it, as they have done already, as an attempt by India to swallow up Pakistan ... Logically and reasonably the only right course for India and Pakistan appears to me [for them] to pull together and yet each one of them having a great deal of autonomy. Perhaps that time will come. But at the present moment any attempt to bring it about may lead to greater ill will and tension.

The ill will and tension is infinitely greater today, so far down the road of unthinking posturing, propaganda and jingoistic hostility have the two countries come.

Kashmir's tragedy is that every sage adviser who comes along today mentions the will of the Kashmiri people only as a necessary afterthought, a token gesture of justice and humanity. India and Pakistan remain the main parties. Short-term pragmatism of this kind needs to be seen in the context of how much has gone wrong in the Valley, which we have ignored to disastrous consequences already. I am reminded of what Noam Chomsky told me during the course of an interview towards the end of 2001. Could there be a solution to the Kashmir problem, I asked. He replied quite simply: 'Yes. Two principles are to be involved—the voice of the Kashmiri population has to be heard and also the UN's call for a referendum. The Kashmir problem took this unfortunate turn after the election was rigged, and till the Kashmiri people's opinion is heard there can be no ready solution.'